Purdy, James.
    Eustace Chisholm and the works. New York, Farrar,
Straus & Giroux [1967]
    241 p. 21 cm.

[3]

I. Title.

eustace chisholm and the works

james purdy /

eustace chisholm

and the **works** /

FARRAR, STRAUS & GIROUX

NEW YORK

contents

I

the sun at noon

1

Eustace Chisholm's street, with the Home for the Incurables to the south and the streetcar line to the west, extended east up to blue immense choppy Lake Michigan. South of its terminus the great gray museum took up acres and acres with its caryatids, and further south rose the steel mills of Gary and South Chicago with their perpetual vomit of fire. Further down his street in a westerly direction, before Washington Park slipped into the colored ghetto, there was a rose garden in which the German poet, Lessing, sat among the blooms.

Here amidst the industrial whirlwind of America's economic burnout, the unemployed, in nondescript small separate armies, with a generous sprinkling of white youths from small towns and farms and up-from-the-South Negroes, stood in line to go on relief.

Eustace Chisholm had been caught up in two tragedies, the national one of his country's economic collapse, and his failed attempt to combine marriage with the calling of narrative poet. He wondered whether it was because of his inability to produce a book or merely the general tenor of the times that his wife, Carla, who had supported him hand and mouth for two years, ran out on him with a baker's apprentice some six months before this story begins.

Eustace answered for his failure as a writer on the grounds that he was too far distant from the great monopoly city of New York, claiming that no Chicago writer could become famous until he had departed the gem of prairies. Yet he dared not ever run the risk of abandoning his coign of vantage on Fifty-fifth Street, with the concomitant danger of losing his native accent and vision, so Eustace stayed in Chicago, where he was known by intimates and strangers as Ace. The original name, like a scar, he reopened each morning while shaving. "I am Eustace," he would mumble into the mirror.

On the day this story begins Ace had been to the Catholic Salvage to see about getting an extra mattress, for Carla had taken the only good one when she had run off. Coming home empty-handed several hours later—the Salvage had only worm-eaten chairs and commodes—he stood a long time at his kitchen window, fingering his shaving cuts, dipping snuff (a habit he had acquired from his young friend, Amos Ratcliffe), and watching some Negroes five floors below delivering kosher meat to a delicatessen. Having come from a small town in northern Michigan some five years before, Ace had still not got used to the sounds of Yiddish in the throats of thrifty merchants, or accustomed to brushing against strange disoriented Negroes, Poles and unidentifiable vagrants in the streets.

Ace was twenty-nine, but he appeared—friends and enemies alike admitted—about ten years younger. Standing at the window, he considered how everybody was going to waste, especially himself. Take his "calling," for example. The only person who was at all impressed by his long narrative poem, written in charcoal stick on old pages of the Chicago *Tribune*, was Clayton Harms, the electric-sign salesman. Clayton, struck by the poet's vague affability and his having a spare bedroom, and suffering seriously from the big-city affliction of unreality and lonesomeness, had moved in on Eustace with his one grip and several cartons of electric signs. His means of livelihood interested and amused Eustace, since Clayton rented his signs to a largely Negro clientele.

Clayton was out late on a service call and in the deepening twilight Ace now sat all alone, writing as usual on his long poem about "original stock" in America. He had turned on all the lights in his apartment overlooking the street and its alley crammed with refuse. He kept all the lights lit despite the expense, as if he wanted to welcome any wanderer who might hit Chicago and give him inspiration, except that these days he knew the lights were really being lit for Amos Ratcliffe. Amos, as Eustace often repeated, clucking his tongue, was in "bad trouble."

In the street below, Amos, a boy of seventeen with a shock of curly light hair, was looking up at the fifth-floor apartment and calling Eustace by name without response. He was about to go into the building and ring the bell when he saw the hulking figure of Daniel Haws approaching the alley.

"Heard you shouting out Eustace's name," Haws said, speaking as if in a kind of grim envy of the boy he addressed. "What are you trying to do, get picked up by the law? What are you calling him for, when you got a place to sleep? Come on home." Daniel Haws, the boy's landlord, was not more than twenty-five himself. Without waiting to see if his tenant followed, Haws strode back to 55th Street, only to run into a young woman with straw-colored hair whom he almost knocked down. He saw her disappear into the front entrance of Eustace's building.

Eustace, finally aroused by the sound of voices below,

pulled up his window and looked down into the alley at the retreating figures of Amos and Daniel. He called out the former's name, but when Amos did not stop he nodded gloomily and mumbled aloud, "That's right, Amos, go home to your landlord. I got my hands full enough as it is. Besides, you'll be back."

At that moment who should open the door without so much as a knock, but his former wife Carla. Pretending not to notice her, Eustace stared in the direction of Amos and Daniel and said aloud: "There go hell and destruction, or my name's not Ace Chisholm."

"How about a cup of something hot?" Carla addressed her remarks to Ace in the manner of someone already at home who extends a thoughtful invitation to a visitor. She rubbed her hands against the cold November night. As she took off her hat, the same old felt she had worn when she went away, she exhibited a pile of straw-colored hair under which a pale peaches-and-cream complexion was fading before the double onslaught of fatigue and mental confusion.

Carla chose the mahogany piano stool, a recent acquisition from the Salvage, and sat down like a pupil waiting for her corrected exam. Eustace looked at her cautiously and obliquely from above his long charcoal pencil. His pallor came and went under his tanned face, and his face and neck flushed angrily a brick red.

"There used to be two and only two things a newspaper was good for—garbage and cat shit—but times have got so bad for writers that I can't even afford yellow scratch-paper. Now I have to use the *Tribune* to write my poems on in charcoal."

"Ace, I'm dying for a good cup of cocoa!"

Her energy made him look her in the eye. "I'm afraid you'll have to be satisfied with some black chicory, princess," he snapped. "We don't serve milk, let alone cocoa, in this house to transients."

She seemed to nod at the word *we* as if to show him she knew he was no longer alone. "May I make us both a cup then of black chicory, Ace?" she inquired.

He nodded ferociously.

She stood up, waited a moment, then began advancing toward him, but he threw his charcoal pencil in her direction, and she stopped.

"But Ace, it took so much brass to come in this door! I *am* back." She held out her arms in an old-fashioned gesture he had seen before only in a junior high school play. He had laughed then and he laughed now.

Beginning to cry, Carla exited in the direction of the kitchen and soon he could hear her cleaning up the dirty dishes he and Clayton had left from breakfast.

"Well, the old thing's back. She's back!" Ace stooped to pick up his stick of charcoal. When he sat down again his gray cat jumped into his lap, and he stroked her absentedmindedly, mumbling, "She's back, Scintilla, when she's no longer needed." But his voice lacked conviction.

"Who's been living here with you, I wonder?" Carla spoke somewhat confidently, even boldly for a runaway, as she reentered the room with two cups of black chicory as per instructions.

"*Who can it be? Not you!*" he paraphrased the words of a popular song, humming and gazing moonily at Scintilla. Then looking in the direction of his former wife, he said loudly: "Some fellow who sells signs lives here, for your information."

"I see," Carla nodded, matter-of-fact, objective from the mahogany stool, but her face, which looked as if it had been slapped, betrayed her hurt and concern.

"But there won't be any question-and-answer period, fine-feathers," he warned her, lash in his voice. "Remember I never answered questions in the past when you were legal here, so don't expect anything generous in the way of info now you're camping on the doorstep unasked and unwanted."

He rustled loose sheets of the Chicago *Tribune*, covered with revisions of his poem, and complained between his teeth about his lot compared with that of the old monomaniac who published this newspaper.

"I'm glad to be back, Ace," Carla told him, trying to keep back tears. "Even if it's only your doorstep I'm allowed on."

"Can you get your job back, d' you suppose?" he talked as if to himself, correcting a word here and there scribbled over the newsprint.

"Yes, I can get a job!" She nodded energetically, under his quizzical stare.

"You'll be needed here to pay the bills, believe you me, Carla, old girl. Shut off the gas a week ago on us. Got it back on now, of course, or we wouldn't be drinking this cup of black, would we? You look bad, Carla, by the way." He studied her coolly. "But except for your hair, you haven't been really pretty for quite some time, have you? You're peeling at the corners, if you ask me. But as I said a while back, we can use another breadwinner around the house. Of course Clayton must have his say about it."

"Have you heard from home lately?" Carla wandered afield a bit. Her eyes had dried and her mouth was set more in the way it had been when she was his wife.

"Aunt Tryphena died last month, in Grand Rapids," he told her.

"She was your favorite aunt, wasn't she?" Carla moved now from the mahogany stool to a small stuffed armchair.

"Next to Aunt Harriet, yes she was," he reflected, putting down the pages of the *Tribune*. "Of course I didn't have the money to go to her funeral," he said and looked accusingly nowhere in particular.

"Oh, dear," she sighed, "I'm sorry," She spoke as if his missing the funeral was connected with another of her shortcomings.

In the long silence which now followed, she got up and touched the mantelpiece and her finger came away covered with the black dust of many months.

"Well, since you're here unasked and unexpected, there's the little problem of where to sleep you." He hesitated. He counted. "I don't suppose you want to sleep with Clayton, in the big bed in the back room," he scolded at the inconvenience of it all, "so I guess we'll bring him out here and sleep him with me on the davenport."

"You're not in love with this Clayton, are you, Ace?" Carla kept back the tears. She was still very jealous of her former husband.

"Oh, when he first moved in we were a bit soft on one another, I'll admit," he sneered. "I've been too busy on these"—he struck the pages of the *Tribune* with open palm —"perhaps always to know where my affections tend, and besides my genius interests Clayton as much as my person."

She dried a tear on the sleeve of her sweater. "It's all my fault, Ace." She bowed her head.

"You bet your goddam life it is!" He began rolling himself a cigarette from a little gray bag of tobacco. "Don't you expect any nice little old forgiveness. Jesus and me don't agree on adulterous women, remember."

"I missed you, Ace, darling, every minute I was gone, say what you will. In fact, I thought only of you the entire time

I was away," Carla spoke in whispers, her genuine way of speaking, even though it sounded like a talking-picture star of the day.

Her confession set him to musing, but he managed after a moment to say: "What you experienced was guilt, then, not nostalgia for me. You're too big a sissy even to enjoy adultery."

He now turned sideways from her and began writing large high sprawling letters on the newsprint so that headlines covered headlines.

Carla had stood up again much in the manner of a schoolgirl who wishes to recite before her turn.

"I feel like the hay," Ace said to his cat, ignoring Carla. "Scintilla," he called to the cat, and when she leaped into his lap, he kissed her whiskers. "Feel like the hay, Scintilla."

"Guess Scintilla is the only thing you love," Carla remarked blankly.

"Carla." Ace now turned his attention to her, employing a kind of schoolteacher lecture voice her own stance had perhaps invoked. "Now you're back, you'll notice some of the regulations are changed. You're back, dearest, let's say, under new house rules. You're here strictly as a breadwinner, not anybody's wife."

"I was afraid it would be this way, Ace." She did try to restrain her tears so she would not anger him more. "But I'm willing and ready to accept your terms." Imploring a little, she added: "But, Ace you don't seem to know why I *did* come back."

"Don't I?" Ace responded icily.

"No, Ace, you don't, and I guess your not knowing why I came back is the reason I left you in the first place."

"Well, do tell." He laughed.

"Will you let me tell you why I came back?" She spoke to him from half a room away.

He scraped some mud off his instep from the bad November weather.

"I came back because I love you, Ace," she said, and a choking suppressed sob punctuated the silence after her remark.

"Do tell, Scintilla," he spoke to the cat as he put it on the floor. "Well, that's your story of course, Carla. Keep in mind the new regulations just the same, if you do decide to stay. Breadwin or get out," he said, removing his clothes for bed.

From the next room where she too was undressing for bed, Carla exclaimed: "Good God, you haven't changed, Ace!" In a low voice, to herself: "And neither have I!" She dried her tears. "I've opened the gates myself and walked right back to the penitentiary," she muttered. "Well, I've been here before, and I can't say I'm unready or unprepared. Worried to death maybe, but not unready."

"In lieu of a nightcap, Carla," Eustace mumbled, massaging his writing-hand under the quilt, "I can tell you right now that if you thought it was hard living with me before, you'll find it damned harder now you're back. Frankly, I didn't expect you to come back, but I'm a little like that mad Jinni rescued from the bottle in the Arabian Nights— now you've come at last but too late to uncork me, I feel this time I'll have to make my rescuer pay. . . . So we'll have none of your dramatic balcony scenes. You're back, Carla love, to take pot luck, you've got nothing that appeals to me this time around, and I don't consider you my wife, owing to you walked out on me, and let me repeat, you're here on sufferance . . ."

"As breadwinner, dear, I understand," she chirped.

"While you were off on your adultery trek, I got this severe crush on a Cuban boxer name of Pete Jimenez. Went to all his matches. Though he's Cuban, I'm sure he has Indian blood, and I'm crazy about Indians, as you probably recollect. I followed him around in the street until he finally took notice of me. Can you imagine then—he invited me up to his room."

Carla began to cry, because boys were one of Ace's failings. In the old days she had never allowed him to tell her about his pickups, at least not in detail, and she must have realized now this would be a subject she would be regaled with indefinitely and with frequency.

"I was so overcome by his physical presence," Eustace went on, "that all I could do when I got to his room was sit in a cramped position on the floor and look at him. He likes to be looked at, so it pleased both of us. Then his brother come in, who is almost a dead-ringer for Pete except he is blind in one eye, and he served us with some kind of a milk drink I guess boxers have to take when in training. They invited me back. Well, any way, even if I never take advantage of it, Pete Jimenez is sure a beauty."

Carla went on crying, which tickled Eustace.

"Why don't you tell me how your book of poetry is coming along?" she managed to say through her paroxysms of weeping. "Or do you only have time now for love!"

"If you had ever developed your powers of observation, you'd see how much progress I made even this evening, while you were making a dramatic comeback."

"You mean that scrawling you do on old newspapers!" She spoke with the vigor of the old Carla.

"If you observed anything at all," Eustace told her, "you would see by the way I put that piece of charocal to paper the progress and advancement I'm making . . . But so far as 'love' is concerned, since you brought the word up," he continued, "I've been hearing that from people ever since I can remember. Some asshole comes into a room wearing pants or a skirt as the case may be, and says, 'Ace, I love you, I love you, Ace,' and then they pour me the poisoned cup, urging, 'Drink this, Ace, it will do you so much good,' and of course you know me, can't refuse a gift, and I take a sip and say, 'But, lover, this foaming potion is poison,' and they answer back, 'You know you don't think that for a minute,' and you know what, Carla, old girl, I *don't* think it for that minute, and they're right. They know me, I'm game for poison and it does me all the good I can get from it. So I always say to my poisoner, 'All right, give me some then on account of I'm game that way,' and they go ahead and give me it."

"Ace, oh Ace, for Christ's own sake, stop, or I'll put on my coat and sleep in the alley."

"Suit yourself." He toned down his voice just the same.

After a creepy silence, Carla's voice came out with: "Describe Clayton Harms to me."

"That's tough to do, lover," he said. "Really tough. I'd just as soon describe one of Mrs. Roosevelt's coal-miners for you."

Carla mumbled, scolded.

"Clayton Harms is a sweet boy who has to be told what to do or he's apt to pee on the geraniums and put the eggs in the toilet bowl for breakfast. You tell him everything he's to do in the morning, and damned if he don't do most of it. He forgets a few things so you can get to scold him for it at night, because he ain't happy unless he's scolded. Or give him a flick of the whip. I've had to whip him several times for not bringing in enough groceries."

"But you little realize money's so hard to find," Carla protested feebly.

"Nobody asked Clayton Harms to come live with me. One night not long ago he come in late-late, with no groceries, nothing, liquor on his breath. I said, looking at the eight-day clock, 'Clayton, where is Daddy's supper?' and he just stood there, blinked, and acted as if turned to stone. 'What kind of liquor is that on your breath, Clay?" I asked, and he wouldn't answer me. 'Expensive, I bet,' I said, and then I ordered him to take off his belt. Oh, how he blubbered, but all in all he was relieved by hearing a more reasonable command than he'd expected. When he had got his belt off, I reached for it like I was all ready to strap him good and then when he was waiting eyes shut to get strapped I spit hard as I could in his face . . . 'That is imported gin on your breath, you fourflusher,' I laughed, and he broke down then and promised me he'd change if I let him stay on."

Just then the door opened, and in came Clayton Harms.

He was a giant of a man, with heavy-lidded large hazel eyes, apple-red cheeks, and a speaking voice almost that of a child.

"I could hear you talking out loud to yourself all down the length of the hall," Clayton addressed Eustace, after switching on the lamp and studying his host's face carefully.

"Guess again, sharp ears." Eustace smiled wryly and then he raised his hand briefly to call attention to sobs emanating from the bedroom.

"Hear it?" Eustace went on, languid. "It's her, my wife come back, she's in bed bawling . . . I don't know whether we'll keep her or not. Depends on how many provisions and things she brings in,"—he raised his voice on the last phrase—"on account of you're getting mighty nonde-pendable and un-providing, Clay, you're all just liquor-breath and promises to do better."

Clayton Harms kneeled down in front of the davenport on which Ace was reclining and said, "Ace, you wrote her to come back, didn't you? Didn't you, Ace!"

"I wrote you to come back, hear that, Carla?" Eustace called in to her.

"Why is she back then?" Clayton Harms wanted to know, getting up from the floor and straightening out the crease in his trousers at the knee.

"I doubt old Carla could tell you herself. Claims it's love," Ace said in a low voice.

"Claims it's love?" Clayton expressed puzzlement.

"Yes, she claims so," Ace said. "Aren't you going to give me my good-evening hug, Clay?" Ace gazed up at the late-comer.

Clayton hugged him bashfully, briefly.

"I don't see why she comes back when we was living all right here without her. Besides she's lost her legal rights," Clayton said.

"Go in there and meet her since we're all under the same damned roof. You can say howdy to her and then forget about her."

Clayton went into the small bedroom where the former Mrs. Chisholm was crying hard now while daubing on her cold cream makeup, and said, "Howdy, Mrs. Chisholm."

"My God, you're a skyscraper," Carla exclaimed.

"Yes, he's tall, thank God," Ace said. "And he looks so average, despite his height. We'd make a nice couple in the summer down on the rocks by the lake."

When Clayton had returned to the front room, they

heard Carla speak for their benefit. "To think he never missed me a bit. Why was I picked to fall in love with somebody who rejects me?"

"Well, it was you run out on him, Mrs. Chisholm," Clayton Harms spoke up, slipping off his high shoes.

"And what good did running off do, I ask you?" Carla took up the question. "He never cared for me here or gone, and he's been rubbing it in all evening how I don't mean as much to him as one of Scintilla's whiskers."

"Well, that's Ace for you, ma'am," Clayton let down his suspenders and dropped his trousers. "You either go with him or you don't, and I guess you and I was meant to go with him, Mrs. Chisholm."

"I guess so, Mr. Harms." Carla's voice slowed with sleep. "Well, nice to have met you . . . Hope you rest comfortable."

"He'll rest the way he always rests—like a log pile, without you wishing the Japanese Sandman on him," Ace yelled at his wife.

Clayton slapped his bare thigh and laughed at Ace's ire, but his laugh unlike his speaking voice was deep, almost bass, and shook the room.

Things quieted down then a bit as if each one was rehearsing what should be said next, when Ace's voice boomed: "Who'll cook my breakfast in the morning?"

"I will," both Clayton Harms and Carla Chisholm shouted.

"Guess I'll have to decide on who tomorrow," Ace said. He turned toward the wall, as Clayton hopped in bed next to him and gave him a generous goodnight kiss on the neck.

"Kiss me louder," Ace said. "I want Carla to hear what strong mouth muscles you have. No, louder still! . . . How about that, Carla? That's the kind of kissing I've been treated to while you were in Kansas City committing adultery."

2

Yawning from above the fan of his urine spraying into the bowl, Ace was already beginning his morning exercises, the practice of which must in part have accounted for his wiry body—he had to keep at the acme for his coming summer appearance on the rocks facing Lake Michigan. As he sucked in his abdomen for the thirtieth time, and contracted his biceps, he could hear Clayton and Carla arguing together while they stood over the gas stove.

Wiping his hands free of tapwater by running them through his thatch of black straight hair, Ace walked out into the dining alcove and sat down for breakfast. After eating the scrambled eggs cooked by Clayton and drinking chicory prepared by Carla, Ace addressed his wife without looking at her.

"I'm having my Greek lesson in the front room at eleven o'clock, so either you stay in the kitchen or better go out. Point is for you to be inconspicuous and unheard. My teacher is even less fond of girls than me."

"Ancient or modern Greek?" Carla spoke with bright strained interest.

"Your memory must have gone down the drain with your good looks in Kansas City. Did you ever know me to be interested in anything modern, Clay?" Ace addressed his friend as the salesman reassembled the davenport from its nighttime into its daytime shape.

"My teacher is a young genius of sixteen or seventeen summers," Ace informed Carla. "Came from way down south in the state, tiny crossroads of a place. But he knows everything. I mean *everything*. Where he got his brains and knowledge in a crossroads—well, the universe is mysterious. And he is celestially good-looking, *too* good-looking for real. Until lately, Clay and I were keeping him, more or less, in food. His grant at the university ran out, and he threatens he'll go on relief. Will lie about his age, as you have to be twenty-one to get handouts that way."

"And how far are you in your study of ancient Greek?" Carla asked with bowed head.

"Oh, isn't someone witty after her long train trip from the West," Ace said.

"Eustace, Eustace!" Carla broke down then, and kneeling on the floor in front of him, she clasped his thighs. As Clayton Harms described the whole scene next day to his paid-up customers, she let out such an infernal hollering that the Irish streetcar conductor on the floor below pounded on the ceiling with a dust-mop handle and yelled:

"Quiet up there, you rotten degenerates, or I'll have the law on you this A.M.!"

Clayton shouted through the cracks in the floor that he was coming down in one half second and break every bone in the conductor's body, but just then the doorbell rang and Ace jumped up and shouted joyfully:

"That's Rat himself. I could tell his ring in hell or on the ocean's floor."

Carla rose from her kneeling position in confusion, not knowing who or what Rat was, or that he was identical with Amos Ratcliffe. She did not even know that no one knew why he was called Rat, except perhaps the name was part of his contradictory character. Everyone said he was too good-looking for an American boy, and yet few failed to learn quickly that he possessed vivid musculature and a hard fist, and nobody made a mistake with him twice. Amos had knocked Clayton Harms down the first time they met, owing to a comment of Clayton's which did not set well with him and which he did not allow as complimentary. Eustace himself, as a matter of fact, was in mortal fear of him. Nobody could be sure on meeting Amos whether he was queer or not, because he was so fierce to approach and those who did so uninvited were injured.

On his entrance, Rat gave Carla Chisholm much the same impression reported by his own Greek teacher back home, a youthful doctor who once described Rat in the words, "The sun at noon—if you do not look away, you run the risk of going blind."

Rat was wearing a large piece of court-plaster across one temple. Ace, after deciding at first it was better not to inquire about it, changed his mind and asked why.

"A fight," Rat replied, puzzled at the disingenuousness of his questioner. Eustace knew the plaster had not been there when Amos was in the alley the night before, and he concluded that Daniel Haws and Rat had had one of their fights.

Carla tiptoed to the door of the room and, almost unaware, stood attentively gazing at the boy.

"Crawl out of the wall somewhere?" Rat inquired. "Whoever you are."

"Never you mind who she is, or rather was," Ace said. "Get in here and quiz me, professor."

"I'd stare you down, lady, but you heard what my pupil said." Rat's eyes burned under the scrutiny given him by

Ace's wife. "Got a pretty good notion too who you might be," he added, a remark that made Carla's face relax for the first time.

After she had gone, Rat scolded Ace, "So this is your woman come back. You backsliding pathic, so you went and sent an S.O.S. for her."

"That's what old Clay charged me with last night," Ace yawned.

Rat came over to within a few inches of Ace's jaw and watched him.

"My God, Rat is lovely!" It was Carla Chisholm's voice again. She reappeared for a moment, ignored by the two men in the room, and was dreamily surveying the scene.

"Get, Carla. I said shoo," Ace mumbled between his teeth.

Rat sat down in the big leather chair with a crash, opened his Greek primer, gave a last blink at Carla retreating to the kitchen, and asked Ace to open his primer to contract verbs on page 38.

"Does he have to do that?" Rat suddenly jerked his head in the direction of Clayton Harms, who had begun sweeping the floor with an oversize broom.

"Clay, knock that off and go to the pool parlor if you got to use your elbow grease."

"Awful dirty in here," Clayton pleaded hopelessly.

"You heard Rat."

Banging the broom into its place in a far corner, grumbling, Clayton Harms trudged on out into the dining nook to sit down facing Carla.

"I have to say it all over again," Carla said to Clayton, but her voice easily carried to the front room. "Never saw such a beautiful boy outside of pictures."

"It won't last," Clayton said in a whisper that did not carry.

"Why not?" Carla wondered.

"Why, he'll die," Clayton replied sleepily in the manner of Ace.

"And where do you get *your* information?" Carla spoke with some of her old wifely authority.

"His palm," Clayton said condescendingly. "Broken fate line."

"Well, I don't need to ask you who's been giving you palmistry lessons," Carla said and sighed, for everybody knew that Eustace could read palms extremely well.

After his father failed in business in Grand Rapids, Michigan, and shot himself through the roof of his mouth in the canning-factory office from which he had conducted his affairs for over thirty years, Eustace Chisholm, two days after the funeral, left for Chicago. The next fall he began attending the university for a while, and actually came close to being graduated. Coming out into the world at the end of the Hoover and beginning of the Roosevelt period, he could find no work except a few parttime jobs that did not last: he worked as a short-order cook in a pullman-car eatery, as a receptionist-file clerk in a home for feeble-minded boys, as a reader to a blind millionaire, and whatever else he could get.

All his jobs terminated, his employers agreed, owing to "something intangible missing in his makeup," and he soon became acquainted with the bite and pinch of full unemployment. Camping on the doorstep of the university vocational guidance bureau, he soon learned the order of preference given to undergraduates and alumni—the bureau was interested first in athletes and lettermen, next in youths with religious training, and third in those with public-speaking experience. Ace's application was always "reactivated" only to be marked after two or three weeks' trial, "not active." He now began the easy descent from intermittently going without to actual deprivation and hunger. He had sunk so low when Miss Carla Hartshorn met him that, when she proposed, he said he had just enough strength left to say yes. Carla made much of her credentials, if nothing of her character as a woman. For that era, she had a "grand" job in the auditing department of the City of Chicago—and she would be able to keep a roof over their heads.

Up to the time he was "saved" by marriage, Eustace had sunk to a low level. He had ended up living with Negroes on 33rd and South Parkway in a "tin house." Along with pennies and cigarette butts in the streets, he had picked up a dose of syphilis, though this badge of Venus surprised him more than it frightened him because of the infrequency with which love had been bestowed on him. The only thing that never failed him in his period of dry rot was the visit of his Muse, for his mania of being a poet seldom left him.

During this pre-Carla period, Eustace Chisholm's fingers trembled so when he lit a cigarette that his colored friends used to inquire if he was sure he was cured, or if he had gone on to locomotor ataxia. Ace would look at his hands thoughtfully in the tin room and say, "Oh, I'm cured of syph but I'm not cured of me. Look at that classic American hand"—holding out his palm—"pure stock from back to the Indians, shaking now like an aspen leaf. No," he would tell his listeners, "I got another bacillus in me science won't find a name for."

Friends of both bride and groom agreed that by the morning of their wedding, Ace Chisholm had certainly crossed the borderline of sanity. In that epoch it scarcely seemed to matter, and Carla had the American woman's fixed idea that love can cure, love can heal, love can bind a flowing wound, and their friends all hoped for the best.

As Carla sat in the dining-nook, three years after their wedding, opposite her husband's lover, the sign-salesman, her thoughts floated round and about the shipwreck of her two marriages, the legal one, and the make-believe one, and she welcomed the presence of Clayton and the progress of the Greek lesson in the front room to keep her from breaking down again with hysteria in front of Amos. Under the encouragement of Clayton's eyes, with the words of Attic Greek sounding like barks from angry whelps, she heard herself talking at length of her hegira, her "adultery trek," confiding all to the ears of a stranger. She made no point of concealing the truth, for the truth was all she could bear now. Her time away had been spent with someone even more impractical than her husband—Baxter Evans—a young man just out of the university, who had found even less of a reception awaiting him in the world than had Ace. He was no more equipped for the one job he had stumbled on, in a big bakery, than he had been for his role as eloper and adulterer. He barely fulfilled his sexual task, and then only because he felt it was part of running away with someone; Ace, of coarser stuff, had at least gone through with the connubial duties, faithfully, regularly, and thoroughly, if without feeling or tenderness. After a few months' freedom, Carla found herself nursing Baxter in cheap lodging rooms, from a sudden onslaught of illnesses which increased in number and symptoms alarmingly: lame back, fever, catarrh, excessive sweating and vomiting. None of the doctors she summoned agreed on what ailed him, and the medicine they prescribed only made him worse. Drinking bootleg whiskey seemed the only palliative, and Carla found herself in strange places and situations trying to secure it. One cold October evening, coming home with his "medicine," she found Baxter gone. After a few days, she was about to go to the police when she became unaccountably ill herself. When she recovered, there was a letter waiting for her postmarked Piqua, Ohio. It was from Baxter's mother, who thanked Carla for having bestowed the most loathsome of all diseases on her son: he was now under the care of their old family physician, but of course he would never have the untainted health he had had before meeting her. She ended her letter with the hope that in the future Carla would insinuate her poison into the bloodstream only of men of her own age and social class and leave promising young men of good family connections like Baxter alone.

Thinking cautiously as she concluded her recital, Clayton Harms raised his coffee cup to the height of the bridge of his nose, in way of salute, and said, "Well, welcome back anyway, old girl!" and winked ferociously at her.

"Just to think," Ace was saying meanwhile in the front room to Amos, "here I am old enough to be your Grandpa, sitting at your feet to get my Greek." He grunted. "I wonder if I'll live long enough to read Pindar."

"You should get as far as *The Greek Anthology*," Amos Ratcliffe ventured, encouraging his pupil with a nice show of teeth.

"Fact is," Ace confided, "I'm not nearly so bright as I was. Don't think I can lay it all at the door of the dose, but you never know. At the time I could only afford the services of a horse doctor, and I'm probably spotty with brain damage, different cirrhoses, kidney attrition, and it would be unsurprising if I now have two or three kinds of blood types inside me what with all those serums they shot through me in charity clinics . . . Only time my mind comes all the way clear is when I'm letting the words run and flow over the Chicago *Tribune*."

"Look over here, Ace," Amos's voice took on an edge. "Do you want your lesson, or don't you?"

Standing up, arching his back, Ace went up to within a few inches of his teacher and inquired, haphazardly, pulling on the lobe of his ear: "What do you do for money these days, Rat?"

Amos Ratcliffe put down his *Introduction to Attic Greek* and now acted like the pupil pausing to answer the professor's weighty question.

Still standing over him, Ace roughed up the boy's shock of tight curls, then touched the piece of court-plaster on his brow, and said: "Who'd you say has been cleaning up on you this time, outside of that landlord of yours?"

The tone of near-concern, touched almost with tenderness, made Rat look up apprehensively.

"I'm not doing *anything* about money," Rat replied to the earlier question of Ace's. "I could go on relief if I was of age, and it so happens I did go over to the welfare office a while back and the minute those relief blacks in the waiting-room caught sight of me, 'Shoo, fly, shoo,' they said and damned if I didn't take their advice and lit out."

Still thinking of money, Ace said: "Don't I remember you once mentioning you had a mother somewhere, an aunt or cousin or somebody."

Amos looked hollow-eyed. "You're thinking of Cousin Ida. That's the name my Mother always goes under, I told you."

Ace sat down and inflated his cheeks like the wind gods

in Italian paintings. "Cousin Ida," he repeated, as Carla made another of her stealthy reappearances at the door.

"Rat's parents were never married." Ace stared at Carla.

"Yes," Amos said sleepily. "I was born entirely out of reference to fucking wedlock."

"So let's cross Cousin Ida off the list of those who can donate funds." Ace wrote something on the fly-leaf of his Greek grammar.

Carla now walked rather rapidly from her post at the threshold to the middle of the room, with a probationary show of confidence and self-assurance.

"Amos, your immediate family then consists only of the person you call Cousin Ida, that is, your mother?" she recited, in the pained metallic voice and would-be omniscient tone of a social-case worker.

Amos stared at her with a blank look that concealed faint amusement mixed with fatigue.

"For instance," Carla almost cooed, "where is your father, at this crisis in your life?"

Amos threw his head back and laughed in a kind of paroxysm which caught even Ace Chisholm off guard. After studying Rat's seizure, Ace decided that it must be genuine.

Calming down a little from his laugh, Rat said, "Your wife must have me mixed up with one of your psychics, Ace, who get asked the whereabouts of missing persons."

Ace sighed uneasily and said, "She's queer on questions today, sure enough." However, his tone was less cutting toward Carla than it had been.

"Well, I don't know what's so funny about what I asked Amos." Carla looked toward Ace as if seeking further social acceptance from that quarter.

"Rat wouldn't know his father if he met him naked in a

shower bath, or stretched out goggle-eyed in the morgue. Rat don't know fathers," Eustace said, rolling on his back on the floor in one of his relaxing exercises.

At this last remark Amos laughed again until his veins stood out in white and green ribbons on his neck.

"Since you have no people to help you, I'd think the university would come to your assistance." Carla spoke with high moral indignation, and then chided the hard times and Amos's bad luck in particular.

Rat shook his head steadily, like a metronome.

"We'll have to find him a millionaire to keep his ass out of the cold this winter, I guess." Ace looked at Amos uneasily, then picked up his Jew's harp, plucking out a phrase from some old song.

"Your husband's a poor scholar today." Amos suddenly came to, jumped up quickly and threw the Greek grammar to the floor beside him.

Carla stood with her arms akimbo, glancing admiringly from Amos to Eustace. It was clear to everybody she was glad now to be home and glad to have permission to remain in the room. "Maybe if I get a job," Carla was saying, meditative in that atmosphere of mixed thoughts and poor attention, "*if*, I say, then perhaps Amos could stay here with us!"

"Ho, a lot you know," Ace scoffed loudly, glowering at her. "Why, Rat wouldn't leave the little nest where he is now for all the jobs you could find in a lifetime. Would you, Rat?"

"Expect not, Ace." Amos suddenly flushed and pounded his fist into the palm of his hand.

"Who is he staying with now, Eustace?" Carla continued, all concern and bright interest.

Amos looked anxiously at Eustace, who answered at once for his friend: "Amos lives with a dirty ex-coalminer, who's a hillbilly and a bully. Ask him to take off that court-plaster to show you how they get on."

At an expression of repulsion and disgust from Carla, Eustace continued his bantering: "Carla can't bear the thought of your curls pressed against a coalminer's chest, Rat."

"For God's sake, we'll have to think of something for him, Ace!" Carla managed to get out, for she had, as a matter of fact, visualized Amos Ratcliffe's case all too well.

"Let's hope," Eustace said, "you'll think up something better for him, Mrs. Chisholm, than you ever did for me."

Carla smiled, brightening perhaps at the fact he had called her "Mrs."

The direful gong of the university chapel tower announced twelve noon.

"About ready for our lunch of hominy and pork butt?" Eustace announced to nobody in particular, then said directly to Carla, "Rat always takes lunch on our Greek lesson days."

Amos yawned so heavily that they were treated to the sight of every one of his teeth and his pink clear tongue.

"I'll lay the plates then!" Carla remembered her place and tiptoed out of the room.

With clenched teeth Amos fulminated at Eustace: "So all the time you were acting like a great old emancipated free body you were tied down to this cunt, who is back, and you're glad of it. Gladness is written all over you."

"That beautiful beautiful angel face and that dirty dirty language coming out of it," Ace said, picking up the Jew's harp again. "I don't know what's going to become of you, Amos dear, unless what your palm says is true, and you'll die. But palms can lie, mark my words. I mean they change, and your death may come by slow freight."

"Dying is the least of whatever is chewing me, you ought to know me that well by now, Ace," Amos said, and at the sudden look of rapt attention on Eustace's face broke into another wild cascade of laughing, partly, as all his friends had long ago agreed, to show off his dimples and fine teeth.

"You shouldn't live with that Daniel Haws either." Eustace mentioned the coalminer-landlord now by name. "Whether you're in love with him or he with you, or both of you with one another, no matter. You've got no future with him. I mean, Amos, do you have to? You ought to live with rich people, Rat. Really and truly. You're a nice boy who's just acting a dirty part. You don't fool me at all. At heart you're really nice, and not who you act like."

Rat spat out a volley of half-hearted obscene expostuations.

"If you cleaned yourself up," Eustace went on poker-faced, "and quit fighting to show people you're not a queer, you might get through the world. Of course, I don't know." He studied Amos closely. "You are mighty special. You're so good-looking and so smart, you're fairly strong, too, but most of your other buttons are missing. Too bad maybe it's so, but so it is."

"Whole country fucked to the dogs, so why single me out, Ace?"

"Most people have their buttons," Eustace continued. "You know what I mean. They get through things without the wear and tear you put on yourself. You're bleeding every step you take. You're crazy, Rat, and you know it, and so am I. Only somehow I'm safe up here with people keeping me, and I'm writing my poem on old newspapers every day. But you're out there all alone with your buttons gone, and so vulnerable." He gave a last look at the court-plaster. "I don't see how you can make it alone, unless you find somebody to care for you."

"Well, we didn't get much Attic Greek took up today, did we?" Amos said as Carla came in to invite them to lunch.

3

Amos lived at the back of a red brick building whose front entrance, permanently closed and boarded up for unexplained reasons, bore the erection date, 1887. You reached Amos's room by going up five wooden flights of stairs in the rear. A stormdoor at the head of the stairs opened on the kitchen used by the landlord, Daniel Haws, as his "business office." Down an interminable hall lighted by a 7½-watt bulb was the six-by-nine cell, furnished with an old Army cot and stool, where Amos was at home with his Greek books.

Whether coal-mining had anything to do with Daniel's walnut complexion or not, Eustace Chisholm claimed that, by living with Daniel, Amos had crossed the color line. Daniel was aware of Eustace's jibe, but the remark only amused him. He said he had always looked dark as far back as he could remember. All year long, even in mid-winter, he looked like a man who had just returned from basking in the Gulf of Mexico sun.

"Actually I don't live with a nigger and Ace knows it," Amos would say. "I live with an Illinois man like me, a lean wiry fellow. Deep wrinkles for so young a fellow, but wrinkles look good on him, maybe because he's all sinew and bones, and anyhow is in a class by himself. He is the landlord of the eight rooms on the top of the 1887 building."

"And the man you have been waiting for," Eustace would reply and Amos would shrug and say, "Amen, Ace, on that." Climbing the stairs now two at a time, Amos smiled and talked aloud as if to prepare himself for the joy of seeing his beloved's face.

The odd thing about Daniel Haws was not his dark coloring, but the striking difference in his character awake and asleep. Awake, he not only never made a single pass at Amos Ratcliffe but seemed to keep a gulf between them all the time. He once said of a newspaper scandal story about two men who had killed themselves over their love that he was opposed to physical relations between members of the male sex, and they ought to electrocute faggots.

The very night Amos moved into the rooming house, the mystery of Daniel was revealed—he turned out to be an incurable sleepwalker. There were no locks or bolts on any of the roomers' doors (Daniel had explained that he must have access to quarters at any time, otherwise they would all be burned to death some fine day on account of the careless habits of his transients), and at two o'clock in the morning of his first night Amos was awakened by the squeak of the opening door. In the feeble hallway light, he saw someone standing on his threshold. The man advanced toward Amos with his eyes open, but the expression in their pupils was so changed that Amos did not at once recognize his landlord. Daniel came directly to Amos's cot, sat down in the manner of a regular visitor, lifted the boy's head casually, touched his hair and, leaning over him close enough for Amos to feel the warmth of his breath, said, without expression or feeling: "Promise me you'll want to stay." A few seconds after saying this, he rose and returned to his own room, having closed the shell of a door behind him.

That had been two months ago. Hardly a night now went by that Daniel did not return, with words and actions nearly identical to those of his first night's visit. Amos knew that his nighttime caller was as different from the daytime Daniel Haws as a dream is from everyday reality. Amos also remembered a description Cousin Ida had given of sleepwalkers: "People who walk in their sleep don't remember a thing, especially where they have walked."

Amos was pitifully aware that the other tenants knew the landlord sleepwalked into his room late at night and he felt sudden hot shame that they knew, for they could construe it only one way; but then, as Eustace said to Amos, "Who after all are the roomers—an unknowable, vague assortment of homeless scarecrows, transients of a night or two." And keeping this in mind, Amos had cheered up considerably, after one sleepless night, when in the kitchen Daniel Haws, preparing him some food "to piece on" between meals, had grinned and said:

"Looks like you're my star boarder, Rat."

And leaving Amos to finish his "piece" on the oilcloth spread, Daniel Haws would go into the adjoining cubicle to do his accounts. One could smell the freshly-sharpened lead pencils and hear the weight of Daniel's Army ledgers as he flopped them open on the roll-top desk.

Had Eustace seen them in the morning breakfasting on the oilcloth-covered kitchen table, he would have conjectured they were total strangers forced together by circumstances, without the slightest trait or characteristic in common. Yet there was one similarity between the cold morning meetings and the passionate encounters of darkness—it was always Amos who looked at Daniel. Daniel's eyes remained as they were when he walked in his sleep—averted.

One morning while drinking coffee with Amos, Daniel Haws looked up suddenly, as if feeling the boy's eyes on him, and said:

"Tryin' to burn holes starin' like that?"

"Guess I was just resting my eyes on you so as not to look at your wallpaper," Amos gave a sour apology.

Daniel closed the book he was reading, a volume of Rhodes's history of the United States, and took a careful look at the kitchen wallpaper.

"Yes," he admitted, "that wallpaper is goddam ancient." He smiled. "But try and buy some new with prices what they are! Even if I was to paper it myself it would break me. Nobody papers his walls with paper anymore, even the rich'll have to quit before long. Know how many wallpaper stores have folded right on this street within the last year or so? All of 'em but one. Maybe a Greek scholar might not know about the cost of wallpaper, but Daniel Haws ain't paperin' his kitchen to please nobody."

After saying this he looked desperately about the room, never once allowing his gaze to rest on Amos direct.

"But I don't know what's come over you the last few weeks, Amos. The way you stare. I won't tell you to stop it, on account of it's probably harmless, but I want you to know I'm aware of it, and I ignore it."

Amos smoothed a deep fold in the oilcloth.

"I like to look at an American face, Daniel," he said bravely.

Daniel touched his mouth with the back of his hand, and shook his head.

"Do you have some little strain of Indian blood in you by

chance, or don't you know?" Amos inquired in a sudden flight of boldness that surprised even himself.

Calm under the onslaught, however, Daniel got out: "Don't know rightly who my ancestors were, to tell the truth."

Daniel rose, pushed out his chest, and having stretched out his arms until the billowing folds of Old Glory tattooed on his forearms were visible through the openings in his sleeves, swiftly strode into his cubicle to occupy himself with tasks Amos described to his face as "doing your arithmetic."

A moment later, suddenly peeping out from amid his ledgers and record books, Daniel taunted: "Stare way, kewpie, if it gives you any pleasure!"

Amos wilted under the remark and turned a dead white. The puzzled landlord looked him in the eye this time, then suddenly angered, wheeled and slammed the door of his office between them.

"Does the son-of-a-bitch know he sleepwalks?" Amos mumbled to himself. But he shook his head immediately. If Daniel had known, he couldn't have made a remark like that. Amos smiled now at the words.

There was another place and time during which Amos could stare at his loved one, unreproved and immune. Every evening for a few hours Daniel Haws got all dolled up and worked as "seater" in the fashionable men's club patronized largely by university professors and trustees. Daniel would stand at the entrance to the huge oak-panelled room, near the cashier, in his black tie, and nod to one distinguished old man after another, usher him to his plate and fork, and then go back to the entrance and wait for the next club member. The rest of the time he spent being the landlord of the top of the 1887 building.

So almost every evening, rain or shine, starlight or fog, Amos walked slowly past the gentlemen's club and paused, looking in. When he located Daniel Haws at last standing there transformed by "evening clothes," Amos felt his heart begin to pound so rapidly that he held on to an iron fence post, while tears came to his eyes. He knew that in about six hours a sleepwalker wearing Daniel Haws's face and body, but with a different soul, would visit him in his cubicle, smooth his hair, mumble words of blind affection, and the visit concluded, stumble cautiously back to his own room for the rest of the sleeping night.

Facing one another now across the dark, here again in the raw November drizzle, only Amos saw and understood. Daniel, looking out into the blackness, perceived only the street-lamp, just as later in his sleepwalking he would gaze at the one he loved with unseeing eyes.

When Amos turned to Eustace Chisholm for advice, Ace said there was no question of doubt that Amos, alias Rat, enjoyed these nocturnal visits more than the landlord. Sleep-walking must take an awful lot out of a man like Daniel Haws, he said, while it gave Amos an excuse for hope and the only kind of love he could accept.

"You're too proud," Ace preached at Amos, "to make any offer of love or declare yourself to anybody. One fine day you've got to give your body to somebody, or turn into a full-fledged zombie. Don't think this is a bid for your favors on my part, incidentally. You're not my type, as the pros say. What if you are only sixteen or seventeen? Old enough to have had your sausage cured a dozen times. Yet you're satisfied with a man who walks in his sleep and gives you a father's touch on the crown of your head."

Offended perhaps by the taunts concerning his virginity,

Amos pulled out a suspicious-looking handmade cigarette and lit it, perhaps to draw attention away from the tears of anger in his eyes. Ace, however, while not missing the tears, took pains to sniff the cigarette, pronouncing it with a condescending sneer, Mexican marijuana, which he called the "schoolboy's consolation."

"You don't give me no credit." Amos offered to crush the cigarette, then thought better and inhaled deeply.

"And all I can say in conclusion," Eustace suddenly warned, "and hark to this: never let Daniel find out he visits you!"

Turning white, Amos mumbled, "Why ever not, Ace?"

Ace smiled, Amos crushed his cigarette, there was the cruel kind of Eustace silence, and then instead of the answer, as was his usual custom, this time there was only a grinding prolongation of silence.

"Well, when you do say something in reply, Ace, don't come up with no more of that talk about his being colored." Amos spoke more out of exasperation at not getting an answer from Eustace than a feeling he must claim Daniel for the white race.

"I have my own definition of nigger and I'll keep it," Eustace said sourly. But his amusement had gone and he warned again: "If you don't do another thing the rest of your life, my young Attic Greek professor, don't let D. Haws know he visits you in the dead of night. Better tattoo that on your fists." Then Eustace lay down on the floor and pulled his knees up under his chin in his "thinking pose."

Scarcely conscious of Eustace, Amos spoke moonily, "Maybe I should come right out and tell him, then."

Again there was a long uncharacteristic silence from Eustace, during which his tongue and mouth moved as they rejected certain words, moved to take others, then rejected those also.

"Maybe, Ace, I should tell him that I love him, I said." Amos forced out the words not looking anywhere, like a blind man who has lost the direction of where his interlocutor has placed himself.

"Well, Ace Chisholm," Amos's voice rose now against the wall of silence, "No cheap cunt-loving cynic like you is going to say that what I feel I am not feeling. I'm not ashamed to say it, I'm in love with Daniel Haws and I'm going to tell him."

"I'll disregard that little old title you just gave me, Amos, on account of it don't describe me to a T at all, and I'm also honest enough to admit I'm afraid of your fists when you're in a state like this . . . But as to your confession of love, Rat, in all sincerity I allow it and I praise it in you."

"I testify to love on account of I treasure love," Amos intoned, releasing the words reluctantly, as a suspect at last admits a crime to some threatening police sergeant.

Coming to a sitting position on the floor, Eustace began creeping slowly toward the chair where Amos had delivered his testimonial, and got directly in front of him where he could look up into the boy's face.

"Christ, you really got it, Amos," Eustace began, "but let an old married friend tell you something straight from the shoulder. You need your Daddy, Rat, and I don't mean me. Your flesh-and-blood sire. You need him, that's the long and the short of it. Why, if Daniel Haws was to take out his naked cock and shake it in your face, you'd die of apoplexy . . ."

Amos played with the loose nail in his shoe sole.

"And if *he* was to find out you were in love with him and

he with you, well . . ." Here Eustace's vocabulary must have failed him for he waved his left hand, and then rose to a standing position, his face averted from Rat. "I wouldn't be in your shoes for a million bucks," Eustace mumbled.

"On account of the death cross in my palm?" Amos grinned deeply, perhaps fancying that he resembled Daniel Haws at that moment.

"On account of that, yes," Eustace replied, "and on account of a lot of things. I feel a millionaire is coming to buy you. Did I tell you—it's told right in your palm also? Then we'll see if Daniel Haws loves you or not. We'll see if Daniel Haws can walk in the daytime too, if it's a question of losing you to a millionaire. Yes, we'll see a lot of history if your palm is telling even a bit of the truth of what life's got in store for you . . . Yes, sir, Amos Ratcliffe, you've a full schedule ahead."

And so with Eustace's warning, "Don't let him find out he visits you," ringing in his ear like some jammed burglar alarm in a deserted warehouse, Amos Ratcliffe drifted on in his situation. He lived only for the late evening visits of Daniel, incapable of rest until they met together on the borderline of slumber. But because Eustace's warnings had made him apprehensive, Amos quailed now under the touch he so desired. His dread communicated itself to the sleepwalker and Daniel Haws, noting a change, spoke more volubly, more uncautiously than before, as he bent over the Army cot.

"What's come over you now when I touch you?" he would complain. Since Amos never replied to him in return, he would look ruefully at the boy with sightless eyes and wearily give him the benediction, "Go to sleep then if you're that scared," and would leave sooner than usual.

4

Stumbling on his way back from his vigil (for a glimpse of Daniel) before the windows of the men's club, Amos ran into the painter, Maureen O'Dell, who acted glad to see him. Her face, from which jutted a nose like Pinocchio's and a vermilion line of mouth, contained a pair of large blue eyes red and puffy from crying.

"You're in trouble, Maureen," Amos volunteered.

Maureen studied him pokerface and did not reply. She had been kind to Amos in a sisterly way in times gone by, had counselled him, and had lent him money which he never returned. She had not seen him since he had moved in with Daniel Haws, and she recalled that it had been at her studio that Amos had first "clapped up a friendship" with Daniel. Though she had been "soft" on the landlord at that time, she had not seen either of them since that fatal introduction.

When Amos repeated his concern for her, "What's your trouble?", Maureen scowled, then regaining her good humor, spoke banteringly.

"I should be mad at you. Taking my fellow away from me." She feigned anger.

Amos looked away sheepishly. He had nearly forgotten all about meeting Daniel Haws at her studio. And as to "taking him," well! He shifted from one poorly shod foot to the other.

Then Maureen laughed her old hearty laugh. "Oh come along, Rat. I'm on my way to Eustace's house. Going to have the whole thing out with him. My sorrow, as you call it. You can hear it there in full . . . and you're *indirectly* connected in any case . . ."

They purposely then tried to talk about indifferent matters, or about topics such as politics and war, and Maureen mentioned that some Nazis were living in her building.

Having arrived at the corner of Fifth-fifth street and Woodlawn Avenue, Maureen pointed up to Eustace's lighted window, exclaiming: "God's got his lamp lit and is waiting for me."

Still snickering over this joke, on the way upstairs, Maureen suddenly stopped, seemed to break down, and grasping Amos's hand and guiding it to her belly, said, "Listen honey, before we go up, old Maureen's knocked up. That's what I've come to talk to Eustace about."

After she had cried a bit more, she burst out into her customary hilarity and laughed boisterously, filling the building with echoes.

"Do you think old Ace will know a good solution?" Maureen asked Amos.

"He's a muller, Maureen, not a solver," Amos said thoughtfully.

Laughing still more exuberantly at his reply, Maureen studied Amos's face carefully and when he smiled at her, said:

"Amos, talk about pearls for teeth . . . you got 'em. No wonder the boys go for you, because I could too and if I had something to push between those pearly teeth I'd be first in line."

Amos drew back from her then not so much because of the wounding effect of the remark as of her breath's smelling strong of whiskey.

"Give old Maureen a nice kiss," she asked, and she began

kissing him inside the mouth industriously. Her hand strayed to his trousers and with professional speed unbuttoned him, pulled out his penis, and fondled it absentmindedly.

"Small but sculpturesque," she pronounced.

When Amos bashfully put his peter back into his trousers, Maureen's laughter again filled the building.

At that moment—they had reached the top of the flight of stairs leading to their destination—Eustace suddenly advanced down the hall.

"A raucous company if I ever heard one!" he sneered.

He looked bilious and quite put out. He was wearing only some underwear and because a draft from the street door blew down the hall (and he had also satisfied his curiosity as to who was making all the noise), he hurried back to his apartment.

When they entered, Eustace was seated on the floor playing solitaire, having flung a Scottish plaid bathrobe about his shoulders. He did not look up as they came in.

"I reckon you two have been out doing the streets together," Eustace commented, studying his playing cards closely. "You two sure can holler when you come up the stairs, especially old Maureen, so that all my God-fearing Irish neighbors get the picture of my life reviewed good so they can report me again to the building superintendent."

Eustace looked up at that moment direct at Maureen's stomach. His eyes lingered there for a moment, then moved back to his card game.

"Somebody's in an ornery temper," Maureen grunted, sitting down in an easy chair with her coat still on.

"I hadn't been informed, however," Ace went on, dealing from a new deck of cards, "that you two cronies were friends again. It always was an odd friendship, but being resumed for a second time like this, I'd call it passing queer."

"Right you are, to call it so, Eustace, my love," Maureen retorted, winking at Amos, who meanwhile had sat down on the floor in a customary pose, and begun as was his custom to feel the sole of his shoe, when Eustace bellowed, "When are you going to go to the goddam shoemaker?"

Then without much change of expression, he called out in the direction of the kitchen: "Better make a few extra cups of something hot to drink, Carla, for unless you're deaf you know we've got company."

"Carla!" Maureen cried in surprise. "Is she back?"

"Everybody's back," Eustace growled.

"Well, I wish you had told me beforehand she was back." Maureen seemed to sober up. "I'd have thought twice about bringing my bad news here tonight. Or I'd thought up a different speech than the one I planned just for you, Ace."

"Oh come off your girly pose, Maureen," Eustace whipped at her. "You know it doesn't matter a hoot in hell whether Carla hears your bad news from you, me, or reads it chalked up on some wall, it won't affect her or you. She has no friends, in any case, so how could she repeat your story except to strangers, and strangers never care enough to repeat anything. So dry up about your sensitive feelings."

"Maybe Carla's return is an omen." Maureen seemed to speak from a sudden recurrence of the blues. "Anyhow I can't tell you, Ace, not now."

"Maureen got herself pregnant, Ace." Amos brought it all out in one of his sudden flashes of information nobody ever was ready for.

Eustace dropped a card, and looked up. He looked at Maureen's stomach again as if to check an earlier impression.

"Here I thought all the time that bulge meant you'd just been on a long beer binge," Eustace said after a few moments silence. "So that's what's sticking out of you."

He gathered up all the cards, put them away in a metal box, and waited a moment, blinking his eyes. It was clear the news had excited him and, because it was bad news, he gave it undivided attention.

"So you'll be out of circulation for a while, Maureen," Eustace finally pronounced. "Don't suppose you know the father."

"Afraid I'll have to disappoint you there, Ace. I do."

Surprised again, Eustace rose, put his arms through the sleeves of his bathrobe, tied the cord tight, and inquired, "And which of your bedfellows out of so many made such a definite impression on you?"

"Rat knows," Maureen said, a deadly coyness in her voice. Her statement caught Amos unaware and he dropped the smiling look which the exchange of words between Maureen and Eustace had occasioned. He turned white as a sheet.

"Rat wouldn't know a father if God came down to show him one!" Eustace cried. "Or have you been hoarding other people's secrets from me, my beauty?" Eustace turned to Amos.

"Well, I'll be damned," Maureen exclaimed. "Rat, the little bastard *don't* know!"

Amos watched her, ashen.

"Father is Daniel Haws of course," Maureen said softly, not taking her eyes off Amos.

Amos rose and went over to the window and looked out.

"Now see what you've done to our little playmate," Eustace cried in glee to Maureen. Then, gravely for him, Eustace spoke up: "Guess maybe you didn't know then, Maureen, Rat is head-over-heels with Daniel Haws and what's more his landlord is ditto with him. There they both are," he spoke to Maureen but addressed Amos, "both of them together hanging by their heels."

"Ace, God damn you," Amos wheeled on him with hard fists and clenched teeth.

Carla entered at that moment with her tray of hot beverage.

Turning toward her, Amos raised his right fist and knocked the tray from her hands, then rushing toward the door which he pulled open with such force its hinges gave a sickening groan, he turned to them to say:

"God damn the whole pack of you!"

He rushed out of the apartment, down the stairs, but they noted an odd discrepancy in the sound of his footsteps, as though a cripple were running. Then Carla, looking down at the damage of the spilled tray, pointed to one of Amos's shoes lying by a broken cup and saucer.

Staring at the shoe which his wife now held in her hand, Eustace advised, "Sit down, Carla, and try to be as calm as Maureen and I are pretending we are."

Maureen had welcomed Carla back with a silent kiss, while with deft quick sleight-of-hand she took Amos's shoe from her, and said: "I'll be back to talk with you both, at length, but before that I'm going after the little snot, and give him back his moccasin. After all, he won't dare leave the building without it in this weather."

Smiling warmly at Carla, Maureen waddled out the door.

Down below, in the vestibule, she found Amos, warming his shoeless foot and his ass against a radiator, his eyes red from angry weeping.

Maureen put her arms around him, but he repulsed her vehemently.

"Put on your shoe, honey," she comforted him. "Then sit down here with me on the steps, why don't you."

Maureen, puffing for breath, had already seated herself.

Having put on his shoe as best he could—it was missing its laces—and giving himself time to pout a bit more, Amos obeyed and sat down next to her.

She kissed him on his ear, pulled at a strand of his hair, and then pressed against him.

"Just to think, we've both been in love with the same guy."

"Don't rub it in, Maureen." Amos pulled away from her.

"I never dreamed you loved him too. I just thought you moved in with him by chance."

"Oh cut it out, will you?" Amos began to get up, but she gently pulled him down again to her side.

"We'll both get over it," Maureen joked.

"Yeah, when we're dead."

"You don't confide in me at all, do you, Amos? You don't confide in anybody of course." She looked at him. "You're adrift in a real sea, kid. More even than me . . . Why don't you trust me a little? I love you for being what you are, Rat, darling . . . Trust me."

"Oh, Maureen," Amos cried, exasperated, "quit harping on it, will you!"

"I understand what you're going through," she went on. He shook his head wearily.

"Let me put it this way: if you'll help me, I'll help you," she began her proposal.

"I don't know how I could help you." Amos scratched his chin. "Can't even help myself . . . Don't believe, come to think of it, anybody ever asked me to help them before." He broke into a laugh. "Suppose I should feel complimented that you think I can."

He took out his box of snuff and dipped, not offering her a pinch. "It reminds me of Cousin Ida all over again," Amos mumbled.

"All right, let it remind you, but help me."

"Sure, Maureen," he said and put his arm around her now. He didn't think she was serious.

"You wait though till you hear what I'm asking of you . . . You can back out then, if you don't want to do it."

"All right, I'm waiting, Maureen."

"Amos, I want you to come with me to the abortion doctor, next Monday."

The color went out of his cheeks, and his mouth tightened. He looked dumfounded.

"I'm not surprised you don't want to. But there's nobody else, if you won't . . ."

He put his arm about her gingerly.

"I just can't go alone," she said, as if to herself.

"I'll go with you, Maureen, so stop fretting."

"I won't lie to you, baby, it'll be awful, really awful. I've been there, after all, before. Can you take it, I mean?"

"If you can take it, Maureen, I can." He was decisive.

"All I need is your moral support, as they say in the movies, hon. You don't have to do a thing but go with me, maybe hold my hand. Baby, you will?"

When he nodded vigorously, she covered him with wet kisses.

"Then we're friends for life," she told him.

He rose now, and walking over to the door rested his hand on the knob.

"I'll have to go back and say good night to Carla and Ace," she said. Her voice sounded relieved. "I'll call you then, Amos, for I know you won't go back on me."

5

More than a bit awed his landlord was to be a father, Amos kept out of Daniel's way the days following Maureen's disclosure, avoiding him except at meals (there being a tacit understanding between them that Amos would starve if Daniel did not give him daily handouts). However, another reason kept Amos shy of seeing much of him: his monthly rent day was coming round and this time Amos had not a dollar to his name. But at last knowing he could not put off a showdown, the boy started walking down the long hall from his room to Daniel Haws's office on the corner of the alleyway, where the landlord received his roomers' rent money.

Daniel Haws always acted considerably different in his office from the way he did, say, when he sat drinking coffee at the big round table covered with oilcloth in the kitchen, or hosting in the men's club dining hall. For one thing, in his office he sat on a tall stool which made the perfect globes of his buttocks noticeable. For another, here he was as disdainful and unhelpful as a drill sergeant.

Today, lingering like a truant before the office threshold, Amos felt that Daniel Haws looked as handsome as a Pawnee brave in the subdued light from the alleyway. Yet the minute he heard Haws say, "What in the blazing hell do you want?" he snapped out of his reverie and knew he had come at the worst of times.

"Well, Mr. Haws," Amos began, but he stopped then, cocked his head, listening to the dripping of the kitchen faucet, then went on with: "I'm behind in my rent as you know." He stepped over to the filing cabinet and leaned against it. "I don't rightly know when I can get any money. As I already told you, my fellowship expired at the university and I can't find a job because of not being registered for classes, and also because of the economic burnout, as Mr. Eustace Chisholm calls it." He giggled awkwardly in the face of Daniel Haws's stony gravity.

A yearning flash of the eyes warred with his angry mouth as the landlord replied: "But being a deadbeat don't interfere with you being able to laugh, does it! Or with that peachbloom complexion of yours!"

He leaned toward the boy threateningly as he spoke, and his Blackwing pencil which he had been holding tight in his grasp, broke unexpectedly and fell to the floor.

Amos stooped to pick up the pieces, but the landlord in angry haste retrieved them.

"Well, do you want me to move out, Mr. Haws?" Amos Ratcliffe said.

"*Mr. Haws*, chicken shit!" he roared at the boy. "Don't you talk up smart to me, you little snot . . . You'll *Daniel* me or you'll call me nothing. I know you, damn you, and you know me. What's owin' the rent got to do with pretendin' I can be Mister to you."

"Then you quit actin' like the Lord and Master with me, if you want to hear me call you Daniel!"

The landlord listened, incredulous, like a traveler who fancies he has heard a familiar voice in a lonesome stretch of woods.

"I asked you do you want me to move or don't you, *Daniel?*" Amos advanced a step toward him. "Well, do you or don't you?" he came close to a tone of command.

Daniel Haws's dimming eyes looked glaucous, almost sightless.

"I could use the room, yes." He mused over Amos's question. He suddenly braced himself against his desk, and threw back his neck into the cupped support of his hands; his Adam's apple bulging out from this pressure revealed itself in full outlines and Amos, watching, lost the thread of the conversation, until Haws, flushing at the rapt pair of eyes fixed on him, exclaimed:

"Christ, it will be a relief frankly to have you and your damned staring puss gone!"

"Well, then, I'd best pack and leave, Dan'l, and you'll have to trust me for the rent, I guess, till I find a job."

"You child prodigies! Why don't you stay home with your folks until the pot ring is off of your ass."

Amos's mouth trembled. Daniel's eyes moved swiftly away from him, lit up suddenly like an idol's from a torch within its empty insides.

"I'll be packing to get, then." Amos started to go.

Haws cleared his throat peremptorily to detain him.

"I don't suppose a scholar like you would be amenable to working around the house for your room," he spoke to the wall behind Amos's back.

"How much do I charge you for your room, by the by?" the landlord inquired, and he took down his ledger from a shelf. As if, thought Amos, the bastard didn't know then and there how much he charged.

"So two and a half is the pitiful sum you're giving for that nice bright front room of mine," Daniel mumbled, looking at the ledger and closing it.

Turning his back on the landlord, Amos rubbed his neck, for he could feel a bad headache coming on.

"Would you mind facing around when I talk to you," Daniel cried.

Amos wheeled about. The look of raw hurt feeling on the

boy's face caused the landlord to halt from further speech for the moment.

"See here, Amos," he began after a silence in which one could hear them both breathing, "give me eight or nine hours of your time a week, doing odd chores, and you can work out the rent for your room."

"Fine and dandy, Daniel," Amos said.

"I'll put you in charge of mopping the floor every morning, keeping the bathroom spick and span, washing all the windows every few days or when there's been a bad rainstorm or sleet or snow. And you can make my bed. Change the linens and so forth."

"Fine, Daniel," Amos nodded.

"While I'm about it, though,"—Daniel Haws looked up wildly at the molding at the top of the room—"I don't mind telling you it don't please me a little bit the way you've been coming home lately. You have this peachbloom face and fancy higher education and yet you live on the street. Come in the other night with one of your shoes off. Hardly a week goes by you don't arrive with a black eye or scratched up and bruised . . . " He looked at Amos now with an appraising indignation as he might have at an expensive piece of his furniture someone was subjecting to ill-use.

"Suppose you want to show the world you're tough in spite of your peachbloom face," the landlord continued, and he paused on the word *peachbloom* as if it was this quality he would tear from all creation. "Well, let me tell you," he pointed a finger, "you don't fight no more while you live here or you can clear out. Get me? Now make yourself scarce on account of I'm pressed for time and I'm behind in my work and don't you come in here again without you knock. Hear?"

"I'll shake then on our agreement, Daniel," Amos Ratcliffe extended his hand. Daniel Haws looked at the proffered hand, a bitter twist on his mouth, slowly extended his own hand, and then with extreme cautiousness took Amos's in his, but without enthusiasm.

"I don't suppose you have any Indian blood in you, do you, Daniel?" Amos Ratcliffe inquired. He seemed to stop drawing in breath as he waited for the answer, but then, to his relief, he saw that such a maladroit question had, if anything, pleased the landlord.

"I'll write the Department of Interior about it." Daniel grinned. He gave the boy then a long look like that of a man trying to recall a name or face he cannot fix in his own complicated memory.

"But I'm not an Indian-giver though, if that's what you're driving at." Daniel went back to his old bitter suspicious tone. "No, sir, when I give a man something, he gets to have it for keeps."

Amos nodded, then taking his leave, walked down the hall. Back in his own "bright front room," he put his head down on his study desk and pressed his eyes against the wood.

6

Some few minutes after the men's club had closed and its lights were extinguished for the night, the millionaire son of millionaires, Reuben Masterson of the North Shore, stone drunk, was being helped down the steps by a cooperative and efficient, if sullen, young man. The helper was not one of his servants, but improbably enough Daniel Haws. The ill-assorted pair were advancing, not in the direction of

Masterson's country estate, the usual path he followed after a fling, but to the landlord's own "roost."

Masterson had arrived at the club fairly intoxicated. By generous helpings from his pocket flask he had become uproarious, then sick, and finally passed out after vomiting on a newly upholstered sofa. The club steward, Mr. Fogarty, not being able to rouse Masterson from the rug on which he lay sprawled, and being too old and infirm to take command, asked Daniel Haws to assist this "scion of a great American family" and member of the club's board to bed—somewhere, anywhere, Daniel's own quarters if possible. Daniel protested, but Mr. Fogarty insisted. He reminded him of the number of young men who would give anything for Daniel's job, and in the end Haws not only complied but came close to saluting as he carried out the order.

Resigned to his task, Daniel walked smartly to the men's lounge, on the floor of which Reuben Masterson still lay stretched out, a deep grin on his mouth, a thatch of brown hair over his eyes. Intent first merely to gauge Masterson's weight and height and deduce how best to carry him to his flat, Daniel paused a moment to study the man in his charge. He grunted with disapproval at what he saw: Reuben Masterson had that indefinable character of wealth about him which the coalminer's son prided himself on always being able to spot—the unconscious man looked too young for his years, there was too much color in his flesh, and too little expression on his pudding-like face—even his wrinkles, Daniel felt, were bestowed on him from fat living rather than by thought or care. Daniel turned back suddenly to Mr. Fogarty, who had stayed at a convenient distance, and put on such an expression of high scorn that the official left the room in dismay. Daniel squatted a moment in preparation, then lifted up the son of one of "America's front families" none too gently, as he might have a side of beef. Masterson, awakening suddenly and struggling to be free, caused Daniel to fix his charge in a kind of modified but savage full-Nelson.

Awakening in this unusual posture was not too surprising for Masterson, who was frequently brought to consciousness in unfamiliar places and unfamiliar arms. He was now partly reassured by familiar surroundings and by the recognition of his rescuer as the personable "host" he had so often nodded to in the club. He had valued Haws, however, as a model of the male servant rather than someone to spend the night with, but now he found the closeness of his presence a more than agreeable sensation.

"Mr. Fogarty has suggested we go to my place, sir, in view of it being so late," Daniel Haws spoke with surly military deference and politeness. He had freed himself from Masterson's embrace, but waited uncertainly at a convenient distance away from the drunk man as he weaved unsteadily from one foot to the other.

"Delightful idea," Masterson complimented him, belching and attempting to focus his eyes as best he could.

"Do you think you can make it, sir?"

Masterson considered the question, then throwing his arms emphatically upwards, cried: "If you'll be around and about to give me a needed hand, don't see why I shouldn't be able to make it again and again!"

Arm in arm the two, after repeated fallings and risings, hoistings and proppings, at last made it to Daniel's alleyway staircase. Then up those unsteady steps, while Masterson cried out in terror as he looked down the sickening height, and Haws's neighbors leaned out their windows and shouted and cursed.

"Never you mind now, sir," was the phrase Daniel had

selected to encourage the reeling man forward, but after hearing it repeated five or six times in a row, Masterson expressed his boredom with it by an acidulous remark which shut Daniel up.

Inside the apartment Mr. Masterson collapsed on the kitchen floor, and Daniel proceeded to make a pot of coffee. He administered it to his guest, still supine, much in the manner of first-aid. Masterson indicated several times he would appreciate his host's sharing out of the same cup, but Daniel sullenly refused.

After more tugging and carrying, Haws landed him on his own bed. Undressing his guest might have been less prolonged had Daniel's amazement not grown with each article of attire he removed. The son of coal miners had never seen such material, let alone handled it, and his resentment of his visitor's wealth was finally replaced by pure astonishment: the imported silk cravat, the hand-stitched shirt with monogram, the pure silk undershirt, embroidered shorts, cashmere hose and Scottish shoes weighing like gold (though probably, Daniel muttered to himself, made of a bull's pizzle), all this finery reduced him at last to sober silence. Stripped bare, Mr. Masterson showed plainly that he had been seriously wounded, one supposed in the war, and these unsightly gashes, together with the traces of what had been an athletic body, counterracted for the moment Daniel's total dislike of him.

Just as Daniel was tucking in Mr. Masterson, the magnate's grandson threw his arms about him ardently and gave him a watery kiss. Drawing back, Daniel wiped the kiss off with slow thorough caution, then somewhat limply set himself down on a small crate he used for a chair. He seemed lost in reverie, or as if reviewing the events of the evening.

"All right, I'm sorry," Reuben Masterson spoke up.

When no reply was forthcoming to his apology, Masterson raised his voice: "See here, Daniel, God damn it, I said I was sorry!"

"People will do anything when they're drunk," Daniel brought out in a whisper, after a struggle to say even this.

"That's where you're wrong, honeybunch." Mr. Masterson turned ugly. "Don't think I'd kiss a brick wall do you, no matter how much liquor I've put under my belt? No, Haws, it must have been something in you made me . . ."

Daniel Haws struck Masterson across the mouth. Masterson let out a cry, prompted in part by the spout of blood which now came from his mouth onto the army blanket covering the bed.

Amos Ratcliffe entered the kitchen just as Reuben Masterson bellowed, and since the door to Daniel's bedroom was open wide, Amos lingered at the threshold, incredulous at the scene before him.

Daniel Haws shot a glance at Amos which combined rage and hatred for the drunk man in his charge, and sudden betrayed passion for the boy at the door. Amos, in exchange, gave Daniel a look of injured trust. For a moment the two men stared at one another with no pretense at disguising what they felt.

Then Daniel's hands fell at his sides, his eyes shifted to the wall.

"Mr. Masterson here became sick at the club, and I was asked to help him," Haws explained lamely, for the first time defending an action of his for Amos's benefit.

"Then all I can say is he come to the right party!" Amos sneered and turned and walked out of the room.

"Amos," Daniel commanded, and in a lightning movement caught up with him in the hall, grabbing his arm and pulling him toward him. "You'll help me with this rich son-of-a-bitch, or I'll know the reason why. Don't act to me like you was keeping a big bank account and could afford to be your own boss."

"Help him yourself. I scrub the floors, not nurse your pickups."

Haws slapped Amos's face smartly twice. "You'll help me, or I'll break you," he breathed into Amos's violently flushing face, then turned back to his bedroom.

Amos stood a moment immobile, his hand making incipient movements to reach up and touch the places where the hard hand had struck him. Then turning suddenly white, his mouth quivering, he walked quickly back into the room where Masterson lay.

Looking up from a basin held shakily for him by Daniel, Reuben Masterson's eyes fell directly again on Amos, entering, and he spoke up thickly but jauntily: "Don't tell me, Haws, we're to be rewarded with a second glimpse of this angel in one night!"

Haws instead of replying removed the basin angrily, placed it on a tiny commode, and began wringing out a washcloth stained with blood, a kind of grim satisfaction on his mouth.

"Daniel, at the risk of getting another wound, may I ask you to introduce me to your god-like young visitor here?"

Haws snorted a kind of laugh in spite of himself and said, gravely apologetic: "I'm sorry I hit you so hard, Mr. Masterson. I only meant to sober you up, frankly."

"You already apologized enough, Daniel, but since you've beat me up you may as well call me Reuben from now on. I don't harbor grudges." Then speaking directly to Amos, he said: "Let me introduce myself—"

But at this moment Daniel interrupted by stepping between them with:

"This is Amos Ratcliffe who rooms here, and, Amos, meet Mr. Reuben Masterson, whose name you must have heard at the university."

Both Amos and Reuben were wonderfully struck by the dignity and poise with which Daniel had made the introduction.

"Now let me bring you some medicine for your cut mouth, sir." Daniel nodded in Masterson's direction, and hastily left the room.

There followed a silence which a casual observer might have thought "embarrassed" but which was explained by Masterson's contentment merely to feast his eyes on Amos and Amos's complete absorption in his violent feelings for Daniel—indeed he was barely conscious of where he was at that moment, let alone of the presence of another person.

"I hate to think what I must look like." Masterson jarred himself out of his reverie and guffawed.

In a still deeper reverie, Amos barely nodded in response to the guest in Daniel's bed.

"Haws spoke of you as being at the university . . . Did he say your last name was Ratcliffe?" Masterson seemed to be trying to recall something, but got of course no prompting. "I'm over at the club some part of the time," he proceeded. "I'm on the board of trustees and such," he laughed again, "but I don't believe I ever set eyes on you before . . ."

Still barely attentive to this voluble attempt at conversation, Amos lifted his hand to the place on his cheek where Daniel had struck him to feel a slight welt rising there and replied: "I'm not in school now, for your information."

"You didn't graduate certainly," Masterson spoke heartily. "Not at your age!"

"Ran out of money."

Mr. Masterson giggled, as if the improbable had been wittily mentioned for his amusement. Then he sat up in bed and shouted:

"But you must be *the* Amos Ratcliffe Maureen O'Dell spoke of some time back. Of course you are!"

Amos looked up now, a bit more attentive.

"Maureen has been promising me an introduction to you for ages, and here we are together before she could plan our formal meeting."

Suddenly, whether from the closeness of the room, the unexpected presence of a guest in Daniel's inviolate bed, or by reason of the sight and smell of blood, Amos felt quite giddy. In order not to fall, he sat down beside Masterson.

Haws entered at that moment with a tray of medicine bottles and some absorbent cotton.

Rising from the bed at the stern look of reproach Daniel gave him, Amos stumbled, keeled over and fell heavily to the floor at Daniel's feet.

"Christ's sake, hospital night!" Haws cried in a strange contortion of voice and features. "Now look at that little bastard, would you . . . "

He kicked Amos with his foot.

"That's about enough of that, you goddam brute!" Masterson jumped up. "You can sock me all you want to but don't you touch him again, or I'll have you locked up . . . How dare you kick him!"

Handing the tray to Masterson with a murderous look, the landlord kneeled down over Amos, who was obviously, he saw, not play-acting.

Something in Daniel's attitude silenced Masterson also.

The landlord lifted Amos up in a kind of ritual slow-motion, this time not needing to compute the weight of what he was to carry, then bore him deliberately down the hall and into his own room. Amos was heavier than he looked.

He put the boy down on his cot, then rose as if in forget-ful confusion over something and shut behind him the door unequipped with a lock. Bending over, he first made the motion to undress Amos, but a shudder of such violence went through him that he had to wait until he could steady himself, then merely put the boy with his clothes still on securely under the blanket.

Suddenly the landlord froze over the unconscious form. A kind of sleep suffused his open eyes. His head bent of its own weight over Amos's body, and his mouth fell heavily and aimlessly across his cheek. At that moment Amos woke up, and seeing his landlord in his familiar sleepwalking guise, did not hesitate a moment to press his face tightly against Daniel's.

The landlord came to with a start, his eyes cleared of sleep.

"Don't leave me, Daniel," the boy cried, terrified. "I need you to stay," he pleaded.

Rising, wrathful, Daniel gave Amos a long uncompre-hending look, then with something like terror he rushed from the room.

The day after Mr. Masterson's departure (the millionaire had remained all day in the grudging care of Daniel Haws), Amos was awakened from a feverish sleep by a surly yell from the landlord, who informed him he was wanted on his office telephone.

So drowsy that later he was not certain how much he had

heard on the phone, or how much he had dreamed when he had got back to his cot, Amos was at least aware that the telephoner was Eustace Chisholm. Since the day he had moved in, Daniel Haws had told Amos that under no circumstances was there to be any incoming or outgoing call except in unusual emergencies, and as Amos now listened to the poet's cascading voice, he was certain that Daniel, bent over his accounts, heard all that Ace was saying.

"Guess who has been visiting me and is here right now," Ace's voice boomed. "It would seem you are in for a change of luck . . . Speak to your new friend Reuben."

They were both drunk, Eustace and Masterson. Terrified of Daniel's disapproval, Amos could only watch the back of the landlord's neck, as motes of sunlight played along his dark skin and fine black hair.

"While the department store king is resting now in my big chair," Ace went on in stentorian tones, "let me tell you straight from the shoulder, Rat, you've captivated him: Masterson. He's made a formal bid for you right here."

"Don't shout, Ace," Amos got out, and he imagined a shiver went through Daniel's spine.

"I said he's bidding for outright purchase," Ace's voice rose in volume. "And because you don't know much about the world outside of Greek contract verbs, let me explain to you this fellow is worth only two hundred millions and though he's been giving me the story it's all tied up in trust funds, I still gather that about a million a month falls on him from some horn of plenty . . . The mystery is how you captivate hearts, child, but that you do it I've got to be the first to admit . . . While your new admirer is out of earshot, let me give you some advice . . . You've got to polish yourself up . . . In cold daylight you might not look so

good to him, or his grandmother, as you did the other midnight . . . Take your credits, first . . . You're handsome,
lovable, smart as a whip, come of good old American stock,
all eyes follow you as you leave a room . . . So much for
credits . . . But your debits, Rat. Hear me out and quit
groaning . . . I can't believe you were in such a bad state
even when you left your Cousin Ida's as you are now . . .
You've gotten common and phony tough and all on account of you will imitate your landlord . . . And where
you haven't followed him, you've done, in most cases, worse
. . . Let's quick take one instance, your landlord wipes his
fundament forward toward his balls. (I know from the days
he came here while courting Maureen O'Dell.) Ditto now
you, as I observe, though when you first went to stool at my
place here prior to your Haws period, you wiped your ass
with a backward swipe like a gentleman . . . You imitate
Daniel also in sucking in your guts (his military training)
until your navel connects with your backbone. This don't
suit your personality . . . But your worst points are not
owing to Daniel Haws. He is the son of a long line of coal-
miners, an ex-soldier, and scrubs himself clean as only a
man who hates himself can—with kerosene and scouring
powder . . . You, Amos, on the other hand, who have ar-
istocracy somewhere in your veins, are dirty . . . Look at
your nails . . . Or your ears, all beeswax thick, or your
downy cheeks, and your neck covered with scurf . . . Only
somebody as good-looking as you could retain your charms
so soiled and grimy . . . What I'm saying is you're not
salable as you are now, so wake up while you've got a lifetime's gold chance."

Suddenly Eustace's voice faded on the wire, and Maureen's boomed.

Daniel threw down a piece of eraser.

"Don't forget our date together, honeybunch," Maureen reminded Amos of his promise to her.

"It's a blowout!" Amos appealed to his landlord.

Springing up from his stool, Daniel, who had obviously heard every word coming from Eustace's end of the wire, strode into the kitchen, where he still kept within earshot.

Eustace now came back on the wire.

"Why should you let yourself go down the drain now, Rat?" the poet's voice boomed again. "You've got everything to bargain with. Will you be a drudge to your landlord when you could be sporting a diamond ring and twelve changes of suits? . . . If you won't look out for yourself, then old Ace Chisholm has got to . . . You adopted me when you began giving me Greek lessons. There's this ancient tongue between us. You don't need a coalminer glorying in his power over you."

Coming into the cubicle now, Daniel took the phone and slammed the receiver down.

Amos stood silently and bent down his head either to show gratitude or allow himself to be cuffed.

Back in his own room, some hours later, Amos woke from a hectic fevered sleep and saw Daniel coming toward him bearing a tray of food. Uncertain whether this was dream or reality, the boy waited, then heard Daniel's full-bodied voice say, "Here's your supper, try to taste some."

7

When "pay day," as Maureen, in her cups, liked to call it, finally arrived, it found her in her studio, whitefaced and mum, completely sober, clutching Amos by the hand. She kept her eyes carefully peeled on the dime-store alarm clock, ticking loudly away. Her appointment with the abortion doctor was in just one hour.

Amos did not try to break her silence. His eyes roved about. Maureen's studio, divided into two rooms, was located on the sixth floor of a tenement that looked out on another tenement as like it as two peas in a pod. The part of the studio where they waited contained her easel, paints, bottles of turpentine, and her bed ("whence all the joy and trouble stems," Eustace Chisholm had said of it). This commanded a central position, and covered now with a handsome flower-embroidered quilt, it suggested a bier.

Amos's own favorite of the two rooms was the one that now adjoined them. Her "waiting-room" Maureen named it because nearly everybody who "waited" there ended up in bed with her. This room contained a collection of ancient rockers, wood statues of Indians and of blackamoors holding rings for horses. There were also her own unsold oils whose subjects ranged from Maureen herself at midnight to scenes of ruined slaughter-houses, pool-room interiors, prairies and corn fields, skies and lawns without depth or perspective. On the floor and walls of the rooms battered linoleum and calcimine, respectively, met in grimy embrace.

Breaking into speech at last, Maureen wondered nervously if this were her third or fourth "pay day" coming up. Liquor had begun to tamper with her memory, she felt, and that was the reason she was not going to take a nip today before going to the "doctor." Of course it had all been Eustace Chisholm's doing, she claimed. He had been her mentor for sexual freedom, had preached and preached she must give herself without stint or measure. Of course he had not been as serious, ever, about her as he was now about Amos and Daniel. True, Eustace had freed her from her Christian Science mother, and from the deadly existence she had led in virginity up to the late age of 23. But perhaps she would have been happier as an old maid in Christian Science, who knows now? Whether, however, it was her third or fourth abortion, today it was somehow her most important, and probably her last. She felt fatality in the air, that's why she had purposely made the bed a kind of flower-covered couch in case it would be the end. She hoped she would die. Anyhow look, she was getting on, she was 27 years old, an old woman by her own standards of judging.

Of all those who had passed from the waiting-room to the workroom in her studio, it was Daniel Haws she had loved, however briefly, the most. Hated him now of course, loathed and detested him. Wanted his blood. Wanted to see him on the cross, and knew one day without the shadow of any doubt, the situations would be reversed, and he would be skewered and drawn and quartered as she was to be today. Yes, that arrogant coalminer bastard must catch it! "But here I am," Maureen observed directly to him, "and Amos honey, look how pale you are all of a sudden." She kissed him.

She reminisced at length about Eustace Chisholm's influence on her life. She had met that bird at a Negro dance-hall which changed its name every few weeks but was called then innocently *The Cotton Patch* and offered female impersonators by way of entertainment. Eustace was unmarried still, she recalled, and he was debating whether entirely to go down the drain of the gay life or allow himself to be kept by a lady who had applied for the post. He had immediately recognized Maureen as his near-equal, certainly a confederate, and had toasted her again and again while a "girl" from the chorus sat on his lap. Later in his den on 33rd Street, in a colored hotel, she had consulted him at length on her future. He had insisted on testing her charms in order to give her the correct advice, but after they had indulged in the act, he told her frankly he was not impressed by her performance, identified her as a "coital repeater" rather than a partner of love, and for all practical purposes still an untrained virgin. He counselled her if she ever wished to become free of her mother and her Christian Science heritage, and if she seriously desired to enter into her own and find fulfilment as an artist, she must give herself unstintingly to the sexual experience and work at it just as she did her painting, in order to discover its secrets. Mind you, she never tired of informing whoever might be her auditor, she had been initiated into the love act at the ripe age of 23 (she had met Eustace when she was 24). With his help and encouragement, she had at last demolished her mother and Science.

As she waited out the hour with Amos, she warmed over her old forgotten rage against her mother (whom she called the Fig); that old dame had withheld any knowledge of the human body from her, had refused to toilet-train her (here she gave the gagging details), and at her first discharge of menstrual blood had been more dismayed than her daughter, and had steadfastly sworn she did not know what the bleeding meant or what to do about it (Maureen had had to turn to a neighbor for assistance and comfort).

Maureen O'Dell's personal tragedy, according to Eustace, was not all to be laid at the door of her mother: Maureen had been born with the face of a gargoyle on the body of a sylph. Having come to a full realization of her predicament, under Ace's tutelage, by the age of 25, she had given up any hope of marriage or an average life. She did not exactly follow her mentor's advice to put a bag over her head and give her body to the first sailor, but she found, once she was "decided," no difficulty whatsoever in persuading any and all young men to mount her regularly. After her "conversion," she and her boys enjoyed themselves to the limit of their endurance, and Maureen became a tried and true successful votary of total sexual intercourse. She was often in bed with a different boy each afternoon, which date was like as not followed by a second tryst with a late-comer for an all-night session. She finally could not get enough of it and with her commitment a kind of strange beauty flowered over her face and body. Many of the young men who came into her studio now took pains to kiss her on the mouth and throat for their joy in union was as intense as if she had been a film queen. Prior to her first abortion she felt herself indeed a beauty. Frequent diurnal coitus was also inspiring to her primitive American painting, and she became well-known (at least in Chicago) for her oils. Her face, as primitive as her work, was recognized on the street, and her role as a "serious fucker" became a mere part of her fame. Her mother never found out, or if she did, was incapable of taking it all in, and she glossed over Maureen's changed way of life, along with her sudden pregnancies and inevitable abortions as completely as she had ignored and refused to comfort her terrified and desperate entry into womanhood.

Bringing to a conclusion her autobiographical diversion, she quoted with relish Eustace's final pronouncement on her: "Afraid old Maureen will never please anybody but beginners, but then of course that's where her big clientele lies, young kids starting manhood. Good for them and good for Maureen. Breaks in our depression boys so they can say they've at least had their bang when nice girls and whores were out of reach."

She slapped her thigh in uproarious laughter.

"Damn old Ace for being such a smarty!" she shook her head.

Maureen took a quick look at the alarm clock, stood up, put on her sheepskin coat, and signalled to Amos it was time to start.

"All you got to do, sweety pie, is hold my little hand on the way there and whistle to fetch me a taxi when I come reeling out from the operation . . . Ain't you lucky to be a boy! No matter who makes love to you, you can go off scot free. Even a dose doesn't keep you off the firing line."

She stared at Amos an unconscionable length of time, then under her breath said: "Come to think of it, though, I wonder which of us is worse off . . ."

Amos's face turned grave, he paled a bit and remarked: "Because I'm in love with Daniel Haws, you mean?"

She made a clicking sound with her tongue. "Or maybe because he's in love with you," she mumbled.

Amos started to expostulate, but she went on: "Well, I'm not jealous of you two, honey, any more," and she kissed him on the mouth. "Let him be in love. Ready now?"

Pausing again she touched him briefly on the cheek. "One last thing," and she appeared to make a real effort now to get the words out. "Don't forget entirely about Reuben Masterson. He's soft on you good, and unlike Daniel, can give you a hand up if he decides to. Should old Maureen kick the bucket, you go call on Reuben, yourself. He's ready for you."

She made a funny face then with her tongue to counter-act the look of trouble which had come over his eyes and mouth, but as he still watched with concern, she grumbled, "Oh, for Christ's sake, I'm not going to kick off, so don't act like you was already weighted down with crepe. You can keep a stiff upper today, if I can."

As they left the white neighborhood behind, and walked into the colored section (Eustace referred to it in those days as "the district"), they abandoned any pretense at reserve, and shared secrets, recent and far-off, fears, and slender ex-pectations.

"Are you sure, though, Daniel's the father?" Amos blurted out, while Maureen was making one of her frequent stops to catch her breath.

"As sure as your mother is of yours," she replied with un-hesitant conviction.

Seeing his consternation at this last remark, she quickly amended her statement: "Oh forget the comparison, honey, I forgot about you and your mother. What I mean is, I'm sure-sure about Daniel. Positive-certain."

She went on: "Imagine that big stiff Haws falling for you." She studied Amos carefully. "I can't be jealous of you somehow because you're not a woman. It's a bit beyond me, but since I had to lose him anyhow I'm glad I lost him to you. Imagine him though in love, even if he sleepwalks for it. He only fucked anyhow to show he was a man. And now see what's come of all his military bearing and army disci-pline. Head over heels with you . . . Anyhow, I don't love him any more and that gives me the strength to give up his baby."

As they neared the abortion doctor's office, situated off

47th Street and Lake Park Avenue, Maureen, never a fast walker, slowed her pace, and Amos slackened his gait to walk beside her until, shuffling and lagging, they resembled stragglers unintentionally bringing up the rear of a cortège.

Their destination stood before them at last, a dingy slate-colored eight-story structure, entirely vacant except for a half-dozen rooms used for obscure purposes, distributed haphazardly throughout the building. They entered the tiny vestibule.

Maureen looked up the black stairwell.

"I think I'd remembered everything about this place except the unimportant little matter there's no elevator, and where we're going is the top floor, wouldn't you know?"

She put her hand over her eyes, and it was Amos's turn to tell her to buck up.

They began the long haul up. The steps were uneven and steep, and the only light came from the same kind of feeble 7½-watt bulb which illuminated the halls of Daniel's rooming house.

About half way up Maureen whispered to Amos that she hoped the baby would come out by itself by the time they had climbed to the top and save everybody all the rest of the bloody bother. But there'd be no luck for her, she said, she'd been scorched before and knew how it went.

"Do the likes of us ever have any luck or break?" Amos spoke with an ancient bitterness she had never heard come from him before.

She observed him for a moment, then shrugging and going up a step ahead of him, said:

"I'm nearly old enough to be your Mother, so I can tell you you'll learn by and by those questions aren't worth the spit to say them with."

Her tone too was one of such unaccustomed strong feeling for her that Amos put his arm around her, and kissed her softly.

They stopped on each landing for Maureen to catch her breath and it was then she cursed Daniel Haws good and hard and thundered for his death.

When they reached Room 889, Amos put his mouth to Maureen's ear and whispered, "What's the Doc going to look like?"

Maureen lifted her finger briefly to her lips, then her mouth directly against Amos's face, whispered back, "Black as the ace of spades and twice as baleful."

"I pictured him before I asked you." He closed his eyes.

She nodded, tightened her mouth, and rapped on the door of frosted plate glass.

A rasping, shuffling sound was heard directly behind the glass, and a Negro of about thirty-five opened the door on them. His hair had been plastered tight against his skull, and he had on a pale yellow pin-stripe suit and was shod in huaraches. A younger Negro with a zig-zag scar across mouth and chin, wearing a silk stocking over his head, stood near the high window blacked out by thick paint. The room was vacant except for two high rough kitchen shelves pushed together to form the operating table, and a small plank with wheels, on the top of which were instruments.

"Is this your young husband?" The "doctor" studied Amos.

"Just a good friend," Maureen replied, nearly inaudible.

"Then he got to leave." The abortionist was decisive.

"Oh, please no, I'll need somebody to help me home!"

"All righty suit yourself." He grinned and reintroduced himself to Maureen, then, in case she had forgotten his name was Mr. Beaufort Vance, but he kept his eyes for a long time on Amos, like a photographer who wants to keep in mind the favorite pose he wants from his subject. After he introduced them also to his assistant, Mr. Clark B. Peebles, he began his set speech:

"Now, Miss O'Dell, should you stop living as a result of this very dangerous operation I am about to perform on you, remember I don't know you, never laid eyes on you. Should you on the other hand recover, which I think you will, considering few of my patients very often die, at least that I ever hear of, then ditto, madame, I don't know you. Clear? Good."

Maureen had kept hold of Amos's hand while Beaufort Vance spoke, and she released it only to undress.

The two Negroes waited in bored impatience as she disrobed. She handed the pieces of her apparel to Amos, who finding nothing to put them on, passed them to Clark B. Peebles; he deposited the clothing in a neat pyramid on the floor.

Beaufort Vance assisted Maureen, mother-naked, up onto the kitchen tables, where once she was stretched out, he gave her face and body a quick inventory, then producing a hypodermic syringe as if out of nowhere, he administered a shot in her thigh.

Maureen made a second request before undergoing the operation—she wanted to hold Amos's hand, and Beaufort Vance granted permission with the bitey injunction to go ahead and enjoy hand-holding all she wanted, for she would be fully conscious throughout the entire proceedings.

Bending over Maureen now, he pulled up her eyelids and looked carefully—it seemed almost angrily—into her pupils.

"Mr. Peebles, where is my surgery tray?" Beaufort Vance raised his voice for the first time. Mr. Peebles gave a cry of apology and alarm, hurried to rectify his oversight, and soon rolled in the little cart on wheels on top of which some dull-colored instruments lay.

Amos, in desperation to know where to put his eyes, let them rest for some time on the surgery tray, a performance which evoked in Beaufort Vance a second bitey remark: "Oh, they're clean enough, never you mind, my very unusual visitor!"

The abortionist, very tall now, stood at the back of Maureen's head. Then to the astonishment of Amos, who was the only one who happened to hear it, having folded his arms, Beaufort Vance beseeched Christ the Savior to bless and guide him in the task ahead.

Opening his eyes from prayer, his face immediately lost its thoughtful look. "Mr. Peebles, where in the flaming hell did you run off to?" he cried. Then locating his assistant drinking from a flask in a far-corner, he gave out a deafening second shout which reverberated through the empty room next to them. "Get your black ass over here, and assume your position at once!" he commanded.

Mr. Peebles quickly ran to the tables, pulled Maureen O'Dell's legs wide apart to lift them to the level at which Beaufort Vance indicated, by a waspish movement of his head, then moving his body quickly to one side, he placed one arm firmly under her knees until she resembled a fowl trussed for the oven. He then applied a vise-like pressure.

Swiftly coming to the fore to face his patient, Beaufort Vance, with incredible speed, began the operation at once by plunging an instrument into the helplessly open, direfully expectant Maureen.

Controlling herself for all of a minute, Maureen then let go with a scream that gave pause to everyone. Beaufort Vance managed to continue exploring with his instrument, but mouthed a command: "Tell her, Mr. Peebles."

Mr. Peebles turned to Maureen and said: "Unless you stop that yelling we got to gag you."

The operation commenced again, but Maureen's screams, even more agonized, soon rose again from the kitchen tables.

Withdrawing the instrument, Beaufort Vance tiptoed quietly to his former position behind Maureen's head, and like a man in a magician act, from nowhere, he produced a gag with tape, and fastened it securely over her mouth.

"We don't want no arm of the law in here now, Miss O'Dell."

Then observing Amos standing by Maureen's side, like a ghost, he seized the boy's hand and clapped it over the gag.

"You can be useful as well as ornamental," the abortionist remarked.

Whether Maureen continued to scream once the gag had been placed on her mouth, Amos scarcely noticed, for his gaze was directed now at the rivulet of blood, mucous, fluid which had suddenly poured out, streaming thickly over the floor.

"The amnion," Amos muttered, horror-stricken, remembering at the same time that the word meant little lamb in Greek. "The amnion!" he raised his voice now as loud as that of Beaufort Vance, but nobody heard him, each intent on work or suffering.

Whether it was the sight of so much blood flowing as far as his shoes, or the strange insane shock that the amniotic sac had to do with Greek for little lamb, the room shot up before him, and then swam in sickening blackness as he fell heavily to the floor.

Beaufort Vance, livid with impatience and anger, bent over him, pulled the boy's tongue out, held a bottle of kitchen ammonia to his nose, then slapped him repeatedly and pushed his head down forcefully. He inspected a rather ugly gash sustained when Amos had fallen. Then seeing the boy had come to, Vance dismissed his cut as nothing, warned him to sit in the corner, and keep his head slightly down, and not to think he was in a serious way.

Squatting in the corner, Amos staunched the bleeding from his cut with a torn snotty handkerchief, helplessly moving his eyes first to the slimy stream of gore circulating under the kitchen tables up to his very position, then to Maureen writhing in torture.

Her cries had become feebler, nearly inaudible, and indeed scarcely human. She vomited persistently through the loosened gag. He had taken so little breakfast he could find nothing inside him to throw up, but retched patiently in sympathetic echo to her paroxysms.

When she no longer made any sound, he watched with fascinated concentration to see if her breast still rose and fell.

At last a cry, ear-splitting and monstrous, broke from her. Her gag came off.

Beaufort Vance's arm, plunged in gore of varying colors, and slime, was drawing out from her body the slashed, battered and decapitated fetus.

Amos vomited freely now, groaning and coughing.

"Bring me that can over there!" Beaufort Vance shouted at Amos. "You, Mr. Faint-Heart, you! March!"

Amos reeled in the direction Beaufort Vance had pointed to with his bloody hands. Somebody, probably the abortionist, had brought a large garbage can into the room, unobserved by Amos.

Amos rolled the can to the place the abortionist indicated, and the latter dropped the bleeding mucous of severed embryo inside, not bothering to close the lid.

Amos found himself again at Maureen's side. His hand sought out hers firmly, but she did not return his pressure.

"The difficult part of the operation is now about to begin, Miss O'Dell," Beaufort Vance was speaking. "So please brace yourself. We are going to scrape your uterus. Ready now?"

Amos placed his hand gently on Maureen's hair, wringing wet with sweat, and resembling under his touch the pelt of an animal.

At an imperious signal from Beaufort Vance, Amos replaced the gag again over her mouth and held it firm.

While the abortionist proceded now with alacrity, perhaps relish, in the final task of the operation, Amos's eyes strayed to the open garbage can, and he pondered that there lay Daniel Haws's son, the proof of his manhood. He wondered if he could ever again look Daniel in the face. He wondered if he could ever again think of love.

However, he was feeling better, if slightly lightheaded, and his nausea had passed, replaced by a headache, which was for the most part bearable, and he tried to keep his eyes from lingering on the gore and horror about him.

Maureen's body, somehow still attractive in its outlines, now resembled that of someone massacred or martyred, unclaimed in a morgue. Her nipples were black, her breasts unearthly alabaster, her abdomen and pubic hair so stained with blood they resembled a huge wreath fashioned out of torn pieces of entrails.

"Oh hon, hon, hon," Maureen moaned under Amos's tender pressure, too weak now to writhe or scream.

Amos gave a last look at Beaufort Vance's arm removing from her body a spoonlike instrument, and noted the muscles of his forearm, suddenly standing out in bulging relief like a page in Gray's *Anatomy*.

Then suddenly, like all terrible things which seem destined to go on forever, this terrible thing was over and done with.

They had been there, not years after all, but only a bit over an hour. As the abortionist pointed out, the time would have been "lots more abbreviated" had Miss O'Dell not been "a 'fraidy cat."

Maureen had asked Amos to fetch her purse so that she could pay for her operation, but when he had brought it, her fingers trembled so badly she could not open the clasp. He opened it then for her, and at her request drew out twenty-five dollars in singles, tied by a rubber band, and counted these into the palm of Beaufort Vance. Lips moving, he went over each and every bill separately, and in fact held up one of them for scrutiny against the feeble light emanating from the blacked-out window.

After pocketing the dollars with the remark that this little transaction didn't need any receipt, Beaufort Vance ushered them to the threshold, and there repeated his earlier tune. "Remember if you die, I don't know you, and if you get well, ditto the same, Miss O'Dell."

Just before closing the door, he gave Maureen a last brief glance, and his face relaxed a bit. "You stay out of the jam jar now for a stretch." Then catching himself looking at Amos full in the face, looked upwards and mumbled, "Can thank our lucky stars no truant officer come callin' for him while we was all up to our ears in our work."

As they walked down Lake Park Avenue in an even more poky manner, if possible, than they had come up it, Amos observed drops of blood falling in slow succession from Maureen's skirts. They signalled in vain for the few taxis which did appear, and almost invariably when a cab did slow down, the driver found an excuse not to take them.

"We're so goddam beautiful they can't trust themselves with us, honey," Maureen managed to quip.

At Maureen's behest—she claimed she preferred to proceed alone now, at her own pace—Amos had run on ahead. In the studio, he turned down her bed with labored care, and began boiling water on the hot plate. After a wait that threatened to consume the remainder of daylight hours, she came puffing in, her hand already nervously unbuttoning her dress.

"Home, thank some weird miracle, whether to live or die don't really matter a tinker's dam." She spoke thickly, an indication she had stopped on the way for a drink.

She let fall her dress, and greedily sank into the open bed, pulling sheets and quilt over her.

Without having to be asked, Amos produced a glass into which he had poured rye whiskey and hot water. He placed the remainder of the bottle on the floor within her easy reach.

"A fifth of this in me, and I'll forget I was ever off my daddy's knee." She smiled at the glass, then drank, finishing it in one huge gulp, then helped herself to the bottle.

"So you got to see how your mother was skewered and eviscerated, scraped and spooned out, and then not even sewed up but sent home hollow." She stared up at the ceiling.

After a long silence she looked over at Amos. His cut had come open again, and was bleeding thickly.

"Yes," Maureen sighed, "I saw baby's broken head." She beckoned him to come near her. "It's not bad, though, sweetheart." She inspected him. In a flash she had poured some of the rye on the cut.

Amos hollered, and she took his hand.

Then after a long harrowing silence, her drowsy voice came out of the deepening shadows: "Why don't you turn on that little table lamp over there next to the pin-cushion?"

When he had switched on the light, she closed her eyes, and was quiet again for a long time.

"Only you would go with me," she began, her eyes still closed, "and that makes us friends forever and a day. Only you," she mumbled, "was man enough to take me and wait while I had my guts scraped. Jesus, why didn't that black butcher scrape my eyeballs at the same time? It couldn't have hurt any worse . . . Be glad you're a man, Amos, even though you don't go for women. Be glad you got a man's thing. There's no future in being a woman after a certain time. Thank God every time you take a look at your little white peter, He didn't make you a woman. Be glad for that all your life, Amos . . . Now excuse me. Mama's going to pass out . . ."

Amos sat on as the twilight turned to heavy black out-side.

When he heard her snoring regularly, he rose, disentangling his hand from hers, gave a last doubtful look about him, and tiptoed out.

8

Years after being mustered out of the army, Daniel went on with his early morning barracks routine. He rose at dawn and took a cold sponge bath, letting the water dry on his flesh as he did vigorous setting-up exercises. He shaved with an old-fashioned straight razor, slapped a coarse smelling alcohol over the abrasions, and then prepared a breakfast of fried potatoes, side bacon, eggs sunny-side up, white toast with oleo, and unpotably strong black coffee. As if expecting military inspection in a tent somewhere in Louisiana, he would then work at polishing his shoes. They were already shined so excessively that Amos once saw his own yellow hair mirrored in the gleaming toe.

Seated at the kitchen table, and only a day or two after Maureen's abortion, Amos waited as usual for Daniel Haws to "finish up" in his office-bedroom. Perhaps unaware his voice would carry all the way to where Daniel was, he muttered:

"What if I was to tell you, Mr. Haws, you were a constant sleepwalker and paid me a visit every night of the week?"

Daniel Haws had just finished going over his shoes with a large horse-hair brush, and his hands hung loosely over his knees. He sat immobile, having heard Amos perfectly well. Then he walked to the kitchen and stopped, staring in the general direction of his persecutor.

"What did I tell you about callin' me *Mister?* And by the way, what was you hollering about to raise the dead in the middle of the night?" Daniel frowned deeply, as if he might begin to remember the night now too.

"You don't aim to answer my question, so I don't yours," Amos replied sadly, wearily. He had planned the question about the sleepwalking, the plan had failed, but Daniel's own question now reminded him too of something he had let slip from mind. During the night, after Daniel had paid his sleepwalking visit to his cot, he had had a bad dream and cried out, awakening himself.

"Your question don't need no answer," Amos heard Daniel's voice droning on. "It's a made-up question besides."

"All right, Daniel, I hollered last night because I dreamed Mr. Masterson asked me to marry him." Amos told the truth, but spoke lightly, as if he had invented the remark on the spot.

"That's a crock of shit," Daniel cried, affronted, even insulted. He turned from Amos as if a grave wrong had been done him. "You haven't put your hand to a mop or broom around here for days," he went on. "Look at the rooms. Filthy!"

But the landlord was unable to bring his usual severity into his voice this morning. Then remembering breakfast, Haws went to the stove, pulled forth the huge evil-colored fry pan, slapped six strips of bacon in it, and going to the window-sill picked up the carton of eggs.

"Why do you say things that don't have no substance in fact or truth, telling me you dreamed that when you didn't dream!" Daniel suddenly cried out. He picked up two eggs, held them in his right hand, carefully smelled them. "Why do you do it?" Daniel wheeled about, and advancing in Amos's direction, came up close to him as if to smell whether *he* was fresh.

Coming within two inches of Amos, he suddenly stopped in his tracks and let the eggs drop from his hand to the floor. Swearing his stream of barracks' oaths, Daniel rushed into the hall, procured a mop, and instead of delegating the task to Amos, went over the linoleum with violent frenzied swipes, howling against everyone and everybody, but somehow offering this time no hint of violence to his star boarder, who remained at the table, petrified.

At the end of his task, however, Daniel turned to Amos and said: "Don't you ever mention again in earshot of me about anybody walkin' in his fucking sleep, you hear?"

"Heard you, Daniel," Amos replied, deathly pale.

He did not dare look at the landlord but knew that the glance the latter gave him was unendurably terrible.

Then in a bewilderingly calm voice, Daniel said: "Now I'll fry us our breakfast."

Daniel Haws's life had come to a full halt, almost an end, when he had been separated under obscure circumstances from the regular U. S. Army. Everything for him since then had been sleepwalking, in one form or another. It was Army ceremonies and routine that he seemed to be re-enacting at many times of the day. Both Daniel and his roomers seemed to be under the distant but certain jurisdiction of the military, whose ceremonies and rituals reappeared at every moment of the day from breakfast to bedcheck.

The strictness of these rules and regulations had finally driven out all but a few "desperate cases," such as Amos, and finally he was the only roomer to remain. None of Daniel's tenants had interested him—indeed he hardly knew their names—until Amos. Unable to take his eyes off the boy's face, he could not admit that the feeling which seized him was love—he regarded it as some physical illness at first. Indeed, from the first beginning and hint of his manhood he had always had girls, had passed for girl-crazy in his family, and had continued his fornications like a good soldier until the present with habitual tireless regularity. He could not feel he wanted the body of Amos (who was a thin boy, though his buttocks had beautiful shape), but he could not deny to himself in his hours of blinding self-revelation that he needed Amos, that it was Amos who dictated everything he felt and represented all he needed. That his whole being was now taken up with a mere boy was simply the last of the long series of disasters which had been his life.

The only things which had held him to life after his separation from service had been his Army clothes, his barracks bag, his shoe brush, and his military routine, until Amos. Even now, alone with him in the empty rooms, he felt that they were in the Army together, and that he was Amos's sergeant.

But this morning the charge that he "sleepwalked" and had visited Amos's room, came as a final unhinging of his self. Rushing out into the street, walking at a gait that was almost a run, he contemplated the thought that he might have "visited" Amos in the night. He remembered that he had had some trouble about sleepwalking in the Army, and it had got on his record. Who knows, he thought, perhaps it was his sleepwalking which had spoiled his career in the Army. Now Amos had brought all the old trouble up again. On that day Daniel walked until sunset, through long stretches of beautified forlorn park, past squatting spoiled Japanese pagodas, shadowed by Moorish apartments built for disappeared millionaires, over trampled peony beds. Ever a victim of melancholy, on this bleak fall day without the faintest trace of sun and under a water-blister sky, he reached the depths of his hell. And all the while only the remembrance of Amos's fair face held him to even a breath of hope.

The scaffolding of his life was falling.

"I wondered when you'd come," was Eustace's opening remark to Daniel, as he opened his door on the former corporal.

"Shit, Ace, I thought I'd surprise you," Daniel Haws said.

"I wish somebody could," Eustace grunted, and motioning for Daniel to follow him, walked out to the kitchen, picked up his spy glasses from the window sill and began looking out listlessly at the inky black alleyway.

Daniel Haws, standing directly behind Eustace, with his hands behind his back in military stance, did not speak. This was his first visit here alone. At other times he had come with Maureen O'Dell, Amos, or someone else.

"Do you think we'll get through the winter, Daniel?" Eustace inquired with dry meaning. He offered him a cubeb, but Daniel refused it.

"Go on, I think you'll need it," Eustace prompted.

Daniel refused again, then, fingers trembling, reached for one.

"I know why you've come, but don't tell me yet." Eustace lit his own cigarette, then seeing Daniel made no move to smoke his, blew out the match.

Putting his cubeb with some difficulty in his pants pocket, Daniel Haws picked up the spy glasses from the sill and looked out into the pitch dark.

"I can't help it, Ace, if you've got second sight," Daniel said, and laid down the glasses.

Taking out a pocket comb from his shirt, Eustace handed it to Daniel.

In sudden self-consciousness, Daniel touched his own hair, usually so perfectly groomed, now disheveled, combed it carefully, handed back the comb to Eustace.

"Let's go back into the front room then," Eustace said, jittery under his calm.

"Well, smarty, since you know why I'm here, tell me," Daniel Haws finally began, looking at one end of his cubeb. He spoke after a silence of many minutes during which time Eustace had been studying a book in French, whose title naturally Daniel could not read.

Eustace slammed shut the book.

"You're the father of Maureen O'Dell's aborted son and you are in love with a faggot named Amos."

Daniel Haws stood up, started to walk aimlessly in the direction of the corridor, down which Scintilla raced, then stopped and smoothed the hairs along the back of his neck. Eustace vociferated, "You have a pair of perfectly chiselled nates. I hope your cock is as well sculpt, and you can sell yourself till the conquerors come."

"I couldn't be in love with a man," Daniel appealed to Eustace.

"What's so special about you?" Ace wondered.

"I've never been, and I can't be now."

"You've never been, and you *are*. And Amos isn't a man, he's practically a child, and nearly as soft as a girl, discounting a few black-and-blue spots and cut mouth and shiner. And he's yours . . ."

The color glowed under Daniel Haws's deep tan.

"He's sick with love for you." Eustace half-closed his eyes like the medium. "So you'd better sop it up while it's flowing because it won't flow forever. No siree. A spring like that is soon dry."

To Eustace Chisholm's considerable astonishment—and he was seldom surprised—he heard weeping, and saw that the big "stand-up-fall-down" (as he called him) was weeping uncontrollably. Daniel dried his eyes, as one would expect, on his fist.

"It's not worth bawling over, Daniel." Eustace rose, something quieter in his voice. He picked up a cup of stale black chicory he had left from afternoon, tasted it, then almost gentle:

"You're too old to be in love for the first time and that's why it's got you hard."

"What do I do, Ace?" Daniel covered his eyes with his palms.

"Tell him you're crazy about him."

"I can't do that."

"Let him tell you then."

"If I had the money, I'd take him with me to some far-off place."

Eustace Chisholm stared at Daniel, incredulous at having heard the last sentence, then, in exasperation, said: "You're in the farthest away place in the world now, mate. You couldn't get any farther away than where you're living with Amos. You're in the asshole of the universe and you don't need to waste more than a half cent of shoeleather to get back. Go home and take him in your arms and tell him he's all you've got. That's what you are to him too, and you'd better hurry, for it won't last for long for either of you, and so why spend any more of your time, his, or mine."

Eustace went out of the room, passed into the dining alcove, and Daniel could hear him twanging on his Jew's harp some dismal folk-song or perhaps hymn.

Out in the street, Daniel Haws walked like a drunken man, now going fast, now slow, stopping to lean occasionally against a lamp post, not noticing or even seeing who passed. Home, he stood in the black kitchen without attempting to turn on the light, near the table at which he and Amos ate.

Then without warning a cry came from his lips. It was a sound that he had perhaps longed to utter since his earliest recollection, back to the time in the coal mines, back to his childhood with his mother and brothers, no, further back, before memory, the cry carried him.

Helpless, in some paralysis of will and mind, he heard

Amos's door open and heard with terror his hurrying approaching footsteps.

A violent wave of nausea came over him even before he saw Amos's face illuminated by a flashlight at the kitchen threshold. His eye was caught by a tiny gold coin strung on a brass chain exposed on Amos's throat where his shirt collar was open.

Hurrying past Amos to the toilet, he did not have time to close the door, but vomited horribly over the bowl, as if now he would part with his guts.

He had not heard Amos's step following behind him, but he felt the boy's cool hand on his forehead as he went on with his agony. When he had done, he raised his head with ponderous effort to look into Amos's eyes.

Daniel Haws, too weak to turn, his mouth still stained from his exertions, stood rigid while Amos Ratcliffe, his own mouth level with his, kissed him deliberately and then, with still more deliberate grave ceremony, wiped his landlord's lips with a cotton handkerchief.

"Leave me be now, Amos, for Christ's sake," Daniel muttered, and his knees buckling, he fell dead weight to the floor.

9

"Even if you're only yesterday's queen, come in," Eustace Chisholm greeted Maureen, his voice rising and falling between impatience to hear the latest tidings, and general stony dissatisfaction with his own present lot. "Set yourself down, but keep away from where I've just been replastering the wall. It caved in on us yesterday night."

Maureen sat down in mock obedience a comfortable distance from the fresh plaster, against the old deeply cracked and peeling portion of wall. About two weeks had passed since Maureen's operation, an event pretty well gone over by her friends and enemies so that her appearance now "back in circulation" caused hardly a stir of interest.

"You look older, Maureen," Eustace pointed out, "as you might be expected to, but you're somehow more attractive than ever before, so watch out . . . Yes," he added, looking narrowly at her, "you've developed a certain air of mystery like old Sphinx Garbo manages to give off."

When younger, Maureen had, as a matter of fact, imagined she resembled the Swedish star, except that Maureen had great firm bouncing breasts. Nonetheless Eustace's comment, rare though any compliment was for him, gave her no pleasure.

"I hear," Eustace went on, blowing out the sweetish smoke of a black Cuban cigarette, and ostentatiously not offering her one, "I hear everywhere that the nigger obstetrician considered Amos the father of your unborn child."

"You hear too good," Maureen scolded faintly.

Hugging her knees with her hands, she mumbled, "If you aren't going to ask me then, Ace, I suppose I'll have to tell you why I really came."

Eustace pricked up his ears then for he couldn't stand secrets.

"All right, Maureen," he chided, "spill it."

"Well, holy ghost," she said, "somebody is starving to death and too bashful to say boo." She indicated the hallway with a jerk of her head.

Ace went outside, where Amos was standing meekly, and took him by the arm and led him into the room.

"You've come, lovers, at a pokey-poor time for handouts," Ace began moodily. "I mean you've picked the worst hell-hole minute in my life to ask me to put on an apron and cook for you two. However . . ."

He spoke in such genuine unhappiness both his visitors showed concern.

"Don't sit there and tell me you haven't heard *my* bad news," he inveighed. "No, I can see by your faces, you haven't."

He stamped out his cubeb on the sole of his shoe.

"Clayton Harms threatened to clear out of here last night after throwing a bookcase at Carla, which I think he meant undoubtedly for me," Eustace told them. "Hence the plaster over there. Yes, Clay said he'll leave me behind if I don't watch my P's and Q's. He give me a dressing-down the likes of which I've never heard of before let alone received. Nobody's seen anybody like him since the Indians. He's a maniac when he thinks he's being eased out. Can't take jealousy. I wouldn't be surprised he's discovered float-ing in the Chicago River one day . . . Anyhow, looks as though romance may be over for me for this winter anyhow, and I'll be settlin' down with Carla to rock-bottom matri-mony . . ."

Maureen and Amos muttered perfunctory words of con-dolence.

"All right, so much for busted romance!" Eustace jumped up, tightened his belt, making an effort, his visitors felt, to look as much like the usual Ace as possible. "Fol-low me on out to the kitchen shelf and we'll see what I can round up for you."

Amos helped Maureen to her feet and they trailed after Ace through the catacomb-like hallway, nearly stepping on Scintilla, who spat lethargically at them.

"That cat hates all visitors," Ace informed them.

In the kitchen their host studied the labels on two cans of bean soup, and finally took these down and opened them.

"My grocery bill is colossal because of dropper-ins like you two," he confided. "At least Maureen can't use the old excuse any more that she's eating for two. But you, Rat, I thought your dream-daddy boarded you . . . Matter of fact I just made a fried sandwich about an hour ago for a young painter name of Al Hall. Hadn't eaten in 42 days, he claimed. Thank Jesus Carla is working again. I had it out with her this morning. 'I'm losing Clayton Harms's love', I said, 'because you returned from your adultery-tour and either you get a decent job and buckle down to business or back you go to Kansas City. I married you so I could have a life of my own, and if you're going to act like any man's American wife and mother, by God I'll smoke you out . . .' She calmed down then and promised to get down to business . . . And another thing I got off my chest—" Eustace stirred the bean soup as vigorously as if it were cement— "I told her, 'Carla, it's not enough you bring us in a decent living, I want you to act glad you're doing what you're doing. I'm the creative one and all the onus is on me to be great. You're the one of whom all that's asked is a bit of oil on the machinery. Kindly do it with a little more enthusiasm. Take off that gray mask that has been you so long and let's see some sunshine and gaiety . . .' She promised me she'd turn over a new leaf then."

Maureen all at once began weeping hard.

"Cripes, what's come over her?" Eustace turned to Amos.

"She has these crying jags now every so often, Ace," Amos mumbled, squinting at Maureen.

Drying her face with a man's bandanna, Maureen managed a giggle, after her own surprising display of feeling, started to speak, could not, then finally got out in one breath:

"My body didn't want to give up Daniel's baby . . . You can put that on your newspaper, Ace."

"That's about the straightest thing you ever said, Maureen." Eustace shrugged. He turned the gas down, then off, under the agate saucepan in which the bean soup had been cooking. He put a tarnished tablespoon in the mixture and tasted.

"Sample this," he handed the spoon to Amos, "and be sure to tell me how good it is."

At nightfall, his guests gone, Eustace sat on the dilapidated Catholic Salvage davenport where he had slept for nearly six months with Clayton Harms, and lighted another cubeb. He felt he might go ahead and bawl like Maureen O'Dell if he didn't snap out of it. His foot suddenly kicked something from under the davenport. Looking down he saw some sort of notebook; picking it up he recognized Clayton's old collection receipts-book. From it emanated Clayton's characteristic odor, which Ace once described as a cross between nasturtiums and gasoline. He picked out the stub of a pencil within its pages, held it tight, and wrote:

"According to Rat, she lay on a kitchen table, looking like a chicken fallen from a barbecue spit while a black hand went in with a ladle and scraped her womb dry. Her mother reads *Science and Health*, don't know her daughter is a whore & walks through shadow of death, and not even

Maureen saw the offspring of her body but her lover's love did, with wide-open blue eyes . . ."

10

Helpless under the punishment which rained down on both of them, Amos turned to—in the landlord's sullen words— "dating" Reuben Masterson. Though Daniel knew that the "whore" Maureen and the "retired queen" Eustace were behind it all, the looks of bitterness he now exchanged with Amos showed that he felt it was all due to their bad luck, which had been with him and Amos from the beginning.

It had begun "for real" one day when the hall telephone rang—a rare event in those days. "Who calls us," asked Daniel, "but wrong numbers and collectors?" Having taken the receiver off the hook and listened, Daniel took it away from his ear, held it against his chest, waited, then still out of breath, called:

"Amos, it's the millionaire juice-head for you."

Closing his eyes while the boy talked and made arrangements where to meet, Daniel steadied himself, knowing in advance he would tell Amos to go.

"You need money desperate, so see him," Daniel heard his own words advising Rat, after the boy had come from the phone and explained Masterson was waiting to take him out.

Expecting something definite from Daniel, a defiant "no" or a blow from his fists, the landlord's "go" was the last of crushed hopes and disappointments for Amos, who stood now, his eyes beginning to fill.

"I'd rather stay, Daniel." Amos forced the words out.

"And go down the rat hole?" Daniel managed a grin.

"Tell me not to, and I won't."

Daniel had heard Amos's final words from somewhere down the black hallway. When the street door had closed on him, Daniel muttered aloud the question that had to await his own answer: "What if the department store heir decides to keep the goods sent out to him on approval?"

He looked at his fingernails, chewed to the quick.

He walked around the kitchen, pigeon-toed, pulled his ears down with his thumb and index finger, and talked cascades to himself.

Daniel thought of the Army then. The word "re-enlistment" came over him like a wave of sea water. He wondered why he hadn't thought of it before. His excitement became so intense he had an erection.

Amos had not told Daniel it was in Maureen O'Dell's studio that Reuben Masterson was waiting to see him. He had also not bothered to mention that Maureen too had spoken to him on the phone and "patted herself on the back" for having arranged the meeting between millionaire and pauper. Both Maureen and Reuben sounded pretty liquored up.

A light powdery snow was beginning to fall. Several times, Amos stopped on the wet pavement, and looked back at his room. Its wretched torn green blinds, absence of curtains, filthy window panes—all to him were as radiant and precious as the lights of the celestial city. He could not restrain himself and finally, leaning against a lamp post—the same one Daniel Haws had leaned against the night he visited Eustace alone—he wept tears as bitter as gall. Nobody but Daniel could have helped to ease his grief, and he knew that Daniel was the last person who would ever help in the one necessary way by admitting his love.

By the time he got to Maureen's, both the "painter-woman" (as she was known amongst her friends), and the "millionaire juice-head" (so known amongst enemies), were in a state of high inebriation.

An array of young men's clothing, brand new, still in their store wrappings, draped over Maureen's bed, immediately caught Amos's eye as he entered.

"Damned if he didn't look right away at his surprise!" Maureen cackled, kissing Amos hard on the mouth. He was somewhat astonished to see that she had on a new gown, an expensive looking ruby-colored necklace, and false eyelashes.

Reuben Masterson made a concerted attempt to act sober, and was extending his hand toward Amos, in his most formal manner, stuttering, "So nice to see you again," when Maureen roared:

"Oh you two fellows have got to kiss now. We can't have this fancy stand-offish front-family formality here, Reubie, for crying out loud!"

"Oh, Maureen," Reuben protested with weak grumpiness, "don't be so bossy!"

"Bossy! Why, kiddy, I'm only trying to live up to my part of the bargain of bringing you two together." She pretended hurt. "You didn't take my talk about us getting married seriously did you? . . . I proposed to Reuben just before you walked in." Maureen winked at Amos with her new lashes.

Refusing to allow Reuben's or Amos's backwardness to squelch her, she pushed the two of them together, and they managed to exchange a few dry kisses during which time Amos's eyes strayed again to Maureen's bed where the new clothes were arrayed.

"We should have put them duds in the next room, so Amos could keep his mind on getting acquainted," Maureen pouted. She fingered her new necklace. "Everybody have a drink!" Maureen shouted. "What's yours, lamby?" she turned to Amos. "Reubie and I are downing our usual straight gin and lemon peel."

"Guess a little bourbon, Maureen."

"Say, you don't sound enthusiastic, angel," Maureen chided. "What's wrong with your eyes? You get bouncy now! Who do you think I arranged this little get-together for! Me? Hell no, didn't you just hear old Reubie turned me down in marriage, though he knows I could introduce him to a million good-looking boys like you."

"Well, Maureen, that's where you're dead wrong, if you'll allow me to say so," Reuben spoke up. "Amos's looks alone make him *one* in a million, but there's a lot more to him than looks, if I know anything about human nature."

"Do tell," Maureen snapped. "Well, have it your own way, Reubie, because after all it's your party, and I'm only the caterer." Maureen could not conceal her growing bad temper. "Supposing then," she motioned to the clothing on her bed, "Amos starts putting on the glad rags you bought him. On account of," she laughed nastily, "his ass has never known anything glad on it before . . ."

"Maureen, if this is all some cruddy joke of yours," Amos chided, riled, while his eye rested on the clothing without real curiosity or desire. "Say now, honestly, whose clothes are they?" he wondered blankly.

Both Reuben and Maureen laughed.

"Well, they ain't mine, love," Maureen cooed, and she picked up the bourbon bottle and refilled Amos's glass.

"Now sometime between sips, kewpie," she went on to Amos, "may I suggest, to get this party so that it bounces just a little bit—I didn't exactly plan a prayer meeting—you start takin' off your old duds, Rat, all of 'em, and while we put 'em aside to burn, you step into the brand new things . . . We'll help you into them, if need be," she added when the boy did not budge.

"Oh let him change in the next room, Maureen," Reuben spoke up, and he walked over to the bed, and picked up the underwear.

"Who the hell is giving the party, Reubie, I ask you, and who the hell introduced you guys to one another? I mean really introduced you. I'm not talking now about you two's meeting at old Daniel's fuck-roost, when you were all so pie-eyed you didn't know who put what up who!"

Amos and Reuben exchanged looks of amusement mixed with pitying contempt for Maureen.

"I said strip!" Maureen yelled.

"It's all right," Reuben handed Amos the underwear, with fingers trembling. "We'll close our eyes while you put these on," he added.

Amos took the underwear and laid it on a chair near him. As if to plunge into an icy pool, he swiftly took off all his old clothes, and too determined to get it all over with, failed to observe that Maureen and Reuben did not keep their promise not to look.

"It brings back to me somehow our visit to old Beaufort Vance, but why, search me!" Maureen appealed to Amos who, as she finished speaking, was naked as a robin, and the center of all eyes.

"Get a load of that complexion," Maureen nudged Reuben. "And that cute rosy little pecker. That's a pecker for the boys to go for, strictly *not* for girls like me . . ."

Without warning, she had leaned down and kissed it. Rising up, she pushed Reuben toward Amos.

"Maureen!" Reuben protested faintly, with his air of what she called front-family etiquette.

"*Maureen* is right," she warned Reuben. "This is my party for you, you dummy, and so everybody got to do like me! That's an order."

"It's all right, Mr. Masterson," Amos, waxen, echoed Reuben's own earlier reassuring phrase to him.

"Now step into that thirty-dollar underwear, for Christ's sake," Maureen exhorted in a tone so astringent that Amos gaped at her.

Although Reuben had just poured himself another double shot of gin, he seemed both more sober and considerably shaken. Putting down his glass, he held the trousers of the new dark blue suit for Amos to step into.

Not liking the drift things were taking, Maureen stepped over to her portable phonograph and turned on a Fats Waller record very loud. When she came back to her party guests, Reuben was just helping Amos into his jacket.

"Well, who do we have here?" Maureen exclaimed, genuinely surprised.

Indeed nobody recognized Amos any longer, not even Amos. His friends urged him to look at himself in a large cracked antique mirror which Maureen kept at the far end of her room, and he gazed without belief at the person reflected there, much as if the unknown mirrored youth might suddenly step out and confront him.

"Talk about comin' into your own," Maureen cried, beside herself. "Reubie, you'll never marry me now, will you?" She broke into angry laughter. "You've turned that little ragamuffin into a fairy prince! Christ, let me look away from him or I might damage my retina!"

She kissed Amos, however, carefully on his cheek and ear.

"Honey, you're still about as clean as a chimney-sweep. I

bet you haven't scraped the wax out of your ears since you left your home town. And them fingernails . . . We ought to scrub our pickups, you and me, Reubie, before we apparel them so rich. Baby," she turned again to Amos, "now you've come into your kingdom, remember dear old Maureen who first introduced you to the upper crust. Boy did I cut myself out when I brought you two together!"

As she said this, Maureen reeled forward, and both Reuben and Amos hastened to catch her before she fell to the floor. They helped her to a chair. She sat back for some time, then speaking like a ventriloquist in a very deep voice, she said:

"You two fellows get out of here and let a lady be private by herself, why don't you. Anyhow party's over . . ."

Placing a hand-stitched quilt over her, Reuben motioned for Amos to follow him into the adjoining room.

Standing by one of the merry-go-round horses, Reuben, more than formal now, nearly funereal, began talking at length to an inattentive Amos.

For one thing, whether owing to the generous shots of bourbon or the shock of seeing himself in new clothes in the tall mirror, Amos had a sense of tenuous diminishing reality, added to which was the heartache over Daniel. But he did hear phrases, as unconvincing or meaningless as all the rest of the evening, coming from Reuben Masterson's mouth when it was not occupied in kissing. It seemed, according to Reuben, that he was head-over-heels in love with Amos.

"I want you to accept these clothes as a gift, but as a gift which is given without any thought of reciprocation on your part . . . I know you are in love with somebody else. I know you are proud . . . You will be doing *me* the favor in keeping the new suit, and allowing me to give you any other gifts which you will be kind enough to accept. Remember, it is the giver who is in your debt, Amos . . . Meanwhile, know that whatever happens, I am your friend. Lean on me when in trouble . . ."

Masterson's high-sounding phrases were succeeded by more kisses, and passionate pressures with his hand down the creases of the new trousers.

"I care for you deeply," the older man said, disengaging his mouth, breathing heavily, "and I can only hope that the day may come when you care for me. Until then, believe you me, you have a friend in me who wants only to help you. This is just the beginning"—he touched the lapel of the suit— "I've already told Mother about you, and as soon as you are ready"—here he paused, perhaps considering how long it would take to get Amos ready—"you must pay us an extended visit to our home in the country, which I hope will become your permanent residence . . ."

A cry from the next room made the statues and bric-a-brac surrounding the two reverberate and creak.

It was Maureen again: "What are you two panty-waists whispering about in there? . . . Who gave you the right to go off and leave your little fiancee, Reubie? Quit loving up Bow-and-Arrows and get in here and pay some attention to little old me."

"Dear Maureen," Reuben whispered in Amos's ear. "She's been so kind, and she's quite remarkable. A wonderful person. And I must confess, dear Amos, I did propose to her awhile back. But nothing now can replace you in my heart."

Amos stared dumfounded at such a simple, open, and unconvincing declaration of love. It had come somehow too late, or at the wrong time and from the wrong quarter to make him feel it, and pulling away from Masterson he walked over to the window, from which he could observe a heavy snow falling.

"Say, God damn it, Reubie, what's afoot?" Maureen's voice came still more vociferous. "Get in here and freshen my glass. You've got lousy manners for the son of a front-family, and just a hour since we're engaged . . ."

"I love you, Amos, remember," Mr. Masterson whispered, and he went into the next room to speak to Maureen.

11

Daniel lost count of exactly how many days Amos had been gone, partly because he did not sleep at all during his absence, so that the elapsed time appeared as day and night merged into one. Later he figured it was only two days and a night.

He found he could not do the work he had painstakingly scheduled for himself—he had enrolled in an evening course in mathematics at the university in preparation for his hope of re-enlistment in the Army—and besides neglecting his books, he failed to show up for his job as host in the men's club.

For the first few hours of Amos's absence, Daniel from time to time would go and stand sheepishly in front of his tenant's room. Had an observer caught sight of him, he might have supposed the door bore a heavy bolt and lock and that the landlord was puzzling how to force it, whereas a mere puff of air would have sufficed to blow it gaping wide.

At last not even bothering to think of an alibi—for deliberately trespassing even in a flat operated by himself gave him pause—he opened the door and walked in. He held his breath as he crossed the threshold. Perhaps he expected to see someone awaiting him there.

With trembling fingers he opened the tiny clothes closet, and once he came behind its frail panelling, in the manner of someone who visits the habitation of a loved one just dead, he held up Amos's few clothes, piece by piece, and finally pressed one of the soiled shirts to his mouth.

Sitting down at the boy's desk, which Daniel himself had made for him out of used lumber, he opened the partly broken drawer and took out a bundle of letters from Cousin Ida to Amos, tied together with a Woolworth red ribbon.

Looking back at the open door briefly, he slipped the ribbon from the packet of letters, studied the dates of the postmarks to see whether they were in chronological order, picked out the earliest of the letters, slid out the single page of ruled tablet paper, and greedily scanned the contents:

"I can't get you off my heart and mind [it began] for I feel you are too young to be living in that wicked great place, with nobody to guide you and the people you write about, precious, are too old and worldly-wise, too lacking in lovingkindness to be good examples. I am surprised your professors take so little interest in you, and why oh why your fellowship was not renewed when you need it so bad, I'll never understand. Come home, Amos, and let Reverend McIlhenny find you something to do here. I know you do not like the church, but you was born into it, dear, and you may one day want to return to it. I do wish you had belief in a Creator, for it would make things easier for you, and it is a rock to fall back upon. I don't think I could get through life without my faith. You can't feel angry with your old Cousin Ida if she goes on praying for you. It may do some good. If I only had money, dearest, I would see you never wanted for a thing. I know it's hard to rise above depressing circumstances and going without, yet we must look on the bright side, Amos, for though these are terrible times, we do have a President now who is trying to do something for us common folk . . ."

Daniel Haws crumpled the paper in his fist, then catching himself, smoothed it out carefully, and replaced it in the envelope.

He stood up, went over to Amos's cot, kicked the legs of it haphazardly, looked at his drug-store wrist-watch. "Come back, God damn you," he apostrophized the absent boy, "or I'll kill you!"

Then unable to resist the packet of letters, he picked up another gingerly, peeked at its firm hand.

Sitting down this time on the floor, he soon was reading omnivorously:

"You remember old Mrs. Henderson who lived down by the refinery. She was found dead in bed early yesterday, had been dead, the coroner believes, for days. Nothing is sadder than lonely old age, that's why I keep busy, dear, and have my house full of roomers . . . If your father had done the right thing by you, Amos—I don't say anything about the way he treated me, but if he had looked after you as a real father should, but he's never shouldered any responsibility to nobody, and I hear he still goes about spending all his dollars on the race track and worse . . .

"When are you coming home, Amos, dear? I've kept your own room ready for you, never rented it to anybody, and it's just the way you left it, with your pictures and books all kept in nice order and dusted . . . I think of our good times together . . . Always remember there is a place here for you . . . But do try to come home, the years are running out . . .

"I worry so, Amos [he turned a page] I don't want to upset you, but the other night I had a terrible dream about you. I thought you had got lost in some woods that looked to me like the old Shaeffer property down by the quarry, only it was now a terrible looking green like maybe in some far-off island, and it seemed something was there that meant to harm you. This dream was so terrible I woke up, my face was bathed in tears, and I was calling your name . . . Don't give it a thought, dear . . . Old age is catching up with me, I guess . . ."

On and on Daniel went until he had come to the final lines of the last letter. If Amos had come in the door while he was reading the letters, somehow Daniel knew he would have surrendered and would have stayed with him and gone crazy and been happy crazy. But Amos did not come in the door, and in a little while Daniel would leave forever.

Just the same he remained in his position on the floor for some time, motionless, the letters strewn about him. He visualized Cousin Ida rising at five to do her washing, tramping about by the morning-glories and sunflowers, hearing the hermit thrush, chasing away all the bluejays who dirtied on her fresh sheets, and every evening, in time for the night train for Chicago, penning a message to Amos . . .

Slowly standing up, carefully putting the letters all back in order, with their ribbon, in the drawer, Daniel looked out of the window to see the lights of the Badger Tavern red in the darkness.

His wrist-watch said 11 P.M.

In one of his lightning-like decisions, Daniel went back to his office-bedroom, opened a battered foot-locker at the base of his bed, pulled out a handful of bills from a huge book that must have been a family Bible, put the money in an envelope and stuck it in his pants pocket.

Without bothering to put on a jacket or coat, he went out into the streets, foul with slush. Shivering in his shirt sleeves, his breath coming out in thick white clouds, he began running toward Lake Park Avenue, head down.

Maureen was speechless when she opened the door on the glowering hulk of Daniel Haws.

"Don't go off on one of your jawing tirades now," he raised his voice sharply.

He pushed the envelope into her hands, warning, "I don't have no time to hear talk . . . I'm leaving Chicago tonight."

He pushed past her, entered the studio, and peered about him, his pupils small and scintillating.

She held the envelope in both her hands, still standing at the threshold. Entering after him, she growled: "Is this a love letter for somebody?"

"Don't tear it up, Maureen," he admonished, edging over to the second room, and giving it a searching glance. "It's money. For you."

Turning about and facing her, he said, "It's a bit late to give it, but better than never. I imagine you can guess what it's for."

She had opened the envelope and now stared incredulous at the number and denomination of the bills within.

"I don't need this money," she said, not recovered from her surprise. She put the bills down on an end-table.

"I didn't want to leave with any debts outstanding," Daniel managed to get out in the face of her growing surliness and anger.

She tightened the cord to her wrapper.

"And you think this God damned noble money makes up for what you put me through?" she exclaimed.

"I told you back then I'd marry you," he mumbled.

"Oh yeah, and you meant that real good and hard, didn't you? Sincere, that's you. Daniel, for Christ's sake." And she let out a cry of exasperation, turning away from him.

"I'm going back to the Army tonight," he said, clasping his hands in front of him.

"Does the Army know this?" she sneered.

He folded his arms now, and his eyes blinked.

"All right, Daniel, what's keeping you then? If you're paid up and your conscience is salved with this dough, get along then . . . Or," she added with savage and unprepared wickedness, "are you hanging around with the hope somebody you half-expected to see here might show up? Well, he's gone . . . Two days ago . . ."

When he didn't budge, she couldn't help going on: "Oh you're not too bad a cuss as they go, I suppose . . . You're one of the strangest men I ever met. No, take that back. You're the strangest. But I know you didn't come here just to give me money and patch up our quarrel, even if maybe you think that's the reason you come yourself."

"Maureen, now!" he cautioned her.

"*Maureen* yourself," she taunted. "You came here about somebody else. You can take your damned money and put it you know where."

Seizing the bills she threw them about the floor.

Patiently he picked up the money and deposited it back on the table.

"Amos is more of a man than you are." She choked back her rage. "He went with me to the abortion doctor at any rate."

Daniel raised his head, astonished.

"Oh, a surprise, huh?" she said. "Well, the surprise was mine when I found out about you and him, let me tell you. Knock me up, and go off with a boy."

When she did not offer to say more, he made a motion to go toward the door.

"You sit down and hear me out until I'm good and ready to let you go," Maureen gave out her order.

"I don't want to stay and hear a lot of shit you picked up at Ace Chisholm's," he protested half-heartedly.

She went over to the money again, and crumpled some of the bills in her fist.

"Mr. Masterson must be generous to somebody these days for them to throw away good money," Daniel countered. Immediately he could have bitten his tongue for having said it.

"I think you know where Masterson is generous right now," Maureen lashed back at him.

"Poor Amos," Daniel shook his head.

"Yes, poor Amos," Maureen cried. "He might have known you'd run out on him, like you did on me . . . You run out on everybody, and you'll never stop running while you've got feet to put to the pavement."

"Sometimes you spare people by running," he defended himself dispiritedly.

"Sometimes you spare yourself more too," she snapped.

"Well, Maureen,"—he looked down at the puddle of melted slush which had come from his shoes—"let me say goodbye then."

She had taken up a glass as they talked, which happened to be filled merely with water, and she came toward him now with it.

"I thought, though," he turned to her again, "I thought

maybe some of the money in the envelope I give to you, well, maybe you could persuade Amos to take a bit of it. I didn't know he went with you that day . . . You don't need to mention who give it . . . Maybe he won't have to stay with Masterson after all . . ."

"If you want to save your little friend from Mr. Masterson so bad, why aren't you man enough to give him the money yourself, and save him yourself. You *love* him, don't you?" she cried, beside herself. Without warning she threw the contents of the glass in his face.

He did not flinch, and there was not a word from him.

"Answer my question, God damn you, or I'll never lift a finger to help you or Amos, if you're both dying in the streets."

She came now to within an inch of his eyes.

"I can't explain it for you, Maureen," he turned violently away from her. "All I know is I have it."

"What?" she screamed, relentless.

"You know," he coughed, helpless. "I love him. I love Amos."

She threw a ragged hand-towel at him then, and he just managed to catch it.

"Wipe yourself dry," she urged. "It's the same towel you used to wipe your come off with here. Been laundered since, of course."

He held the towel for some time before his face without touching it to him, then swiftly pressed it against his flesh.

She wheeled away from him. "All I've been treated to for the last six months is stories about guys in love with guys. Christ, the age of anybody being in love with girls must be over! We're as useless as warts on a frog."

The water from her glass still glistened on his face like

tears, as she looked up at him again, but she knew Daniel, if he could weep, would shed sorrow dry as stone.

"Oh, I'll do what I can for your little friend," she spoke after a bit. "But I'll do it for his sake, not yours . . . You'd best to leave now, Daniel. Somebody's coming to see me in a few minutes."

She looked quickly toward her bed.

He didn't budge and she did not press him.

"Why can't you tell Amos, though, before you go what you just now told me?" Her anger came up again briefly. "Why can't you, Daniel?" she asked, relenting a bit.

"Why don't you ask God?" he shot at her, turned, and opened the door.

She couldn't forget the look on his face. It was not, she realized, Daniel's face any more. It was not the face of any man she had ever seen.

"You're really off for the Army then?" She had come out into the corridor to call after him.

"In a few hours." He spoke with his back to her, then disappeared down the stairwell.

II

in distortion-free mirrors

12

PUBLIC AUCTION
Goods & Furnishings from the Rooms
Top of 1887 Building
December 12, 10:00 A.M.

Standing motionless for some time before this sign attached
to a lamp post, Eustace exclaimed. "So then the birds are
flown!"

Nonetheless he had hurried to the alley and up the back
staircase in some faint hope of finding the landlord if not
the tenant, but he arrived only in time for the perfunctory
conclusion of the auction itself: the few people in attendance were already leaving with the sticks, boards, and vessels which passed for furniture, a water pitcher, a broken
bookcase, or a small mirror under somebody's arm—articles
which a later epoch would hardly deem worthy of the
dump-heap.

But in a far corner, Eustace caught sight of paper—old
letters, ledgers—and it was paper, as he had once joked to
Amos, that he was really queer for. The auctioneer, about
to follow the congregation down the staircase, observed the
poet's interest, stepped over to him cautiously, and after
convincing himself that the would-be purchaser was as im-

pecunious as he appeared, sold him all the "trash" for twenty-five cents, which Eustace counted out into the fellow's mittened hand in uneven change, mostly pennies.

Only when Ace had the bundle of papers in his own room did he realize the magnitude of his luck (and his loss). He found himself in possession not only of Cousin Ida's letters, but Amos's scrawled notes to himself on his Greek lessons. But the find of finds was a diary of Daniel Haws scribbled in an old record-book of rents due and problems in trigonometry. Among the pile he also found a recent letter, yet unopened, from Cousin Ida to Amos. But with his joy over treasure came the realization that the two men to whom the papers belonged were gone, probably forever. To Eustace it seemed unlikely he would ever set eyes on either of them again.

About a week after the auction, Carla brought Eustace a red-white-and-blue envelope with an Army A. P. O. address, and said, "Who are you exchanging information with in the armed forces?"

"Jesus, he's done it," Ace cried, after glancing through a sheaf of ruled letter paper extricated from the envelope. "It's our landlord-hero, Daniel Haws."

Some people confess in the flesh, others on paper. Daniel, a mumbler or a mute in company, could pour himself out on a blank sheet of paper in a P. X. waiting-room to an invisible correspondent.

His choice of Ace as a correspondent came about soon after he was inducted into the Army. Daniel went first through Camp Grant, thence to the baked plains of Scott Field, and finally to Biloxi, Mississippi where, one grim Sunday morning, seated at a table in the P. X., he heard the voice of a chaplain addressing him.

"Attending chapel today, soldier?"

When Daniel claimed no church, the chaplain went on, "Then, son, do the next best thing and write home."

"Nobody left to home, sir," he replied.

"You've talked with Captain Stadger, I suppose." The chaplan studied Daniel's face carefully.

Daniel paused over the name, and his eyes blinked.

"That's all right," the chaplain cleared his throat. "You look like a capable young fellow and probably ought to go into special training school . . . I'll let the captain know about you. But write to somebody, today." He pointed to letter-paper and enveolpes laid out on the stand beside them.

When the chaplain had departed, Daniel looked about the room, saw that four or five other soldiers were busy with letter-writing. A sign often seen in flophouses and other lodgings of desperation was hanging on the wall:

HAVE YOU WRITTEN HOME
TO HER TODAY?

Starting suddenly, as if he were just hearing the name *Captain Stadger* minutes after the chaplain had pronounced it to him, Daniel gave a short low cry and laid his head down against the writing arm of the chair.

Unable to call to mind what disturbed him, he groped now to find his bearings. His body knew something which he could not define, and it had cried out just now with his voice.

What Daniel Haws could not tell himself, because he did not remember, was that on the very first night of his arrival in camp, he had sleepwalked into the tent of Captain

Stadger. The officer, still awake at 2:30 A.M. and swatting from time to time at a moth which flew about his only illumination, a flashlight, was occupied in rubbing salve into a ringworm on his arm. He looked up with unbelief and yet with an expression of recognition and fulfilled hope at the sight of the soldier standing stark naked with sightless eyes before him.

Rising, pointing his flashlight away from the soldier's face and over his body, the captain studied and waited. Then sensing what he had on his hands, he quickly looked at the serial number on the sleepwalker's dog-tag and in a hollow voice of command, in strict military etiquette, dismissed his caller with the implication that it had been the captain who had summoned him from his tent and would summon him again. Obedient, Daniel saluted and, with still unseeing eyes, pivoted and with steady bearing marched back to his cot.

Shaken by something half-remembered and by the name of his captain, and unwelcome as the very sound *Eustace Chisholm* was to him, nonetheless Daniel's fingers, pressed white against the leadpencil, began to move over the letter-paper as he wrote a message to Chicago:

"Why, Ace, you will ask," Daniel Haws wrote, "am I sending this letter to you. Well, that is a question I might better put to myself. I have lost all shame. Spreading the cheeks of my ass for every little graduate 2nd lieutenant from West Point to look up, milking my cock in short-arm inspection, cleaning garbage cans, having my arms and thighs shot full of cow-pox and typhoid, I am a public mop-handle, they have all of me, and are planning to sever anything they cannot freely manipulate. Since I have lost all shame here in Mississippi and since you never had any, and I know you blab everything the minute you hear it, for though you are people say brilliant, you are the lowest species of human being ever crawled over earth, and you will admit this, for if there is one thing in you that distinguishes you from slime it is you are honest, this makes you I imagine, a man. I admire the trait and you are the one I can write to as a consequence. You are a chancre and you admit it. I do not know what I am, the only thing I know is I signed back to hell, can you figure it out, nobody here can—I was in this hell once and came back of my own free will to reenlist at the advanced age of 25, but as I said I have no shame and will admit to you on paper, which you can show then to all your cackling ball-less friends that what I have I have bad, the fever of Amos, I mean. I ran away thinking I would get it out of my blood but my blood now is burning like naphtha. I have broken the rules here and gone out of bounds nightly to the nigger whorehouse and every black whore I have been with only brought out the fire of Amos and burned me to the root of my insides with it. I am in love with him and can only admit it to a hyena like you. If there was God for me, I would be on my knees all day, all night, I would have entered a religious order, but there is no-nothing for me but Amos, and now the army—I need it, and the army I can see sees I need it. I am under, I understand, a Captain Stadger, who is death in circles, and I hear from beforehand he will exercise all the authority he has over me, well, let him, let him put me on the wheel if he has to and twist until I recognize the authority of the army so good there will be nothing but it over me, over and above Amos and even all the pain—Give me news of him. I earn only twenty bucks a month but am willing to give it all to you for word from that curly-haired master of me. I will even beg, borrow and steal to give you more, if you will only write me about him. Ace, I'm on my knees in front of you. DANIEL HAWS, Head-quarters Squad, Biloxi, Miss."

Stunned perhaps as much by his unexpected luck as at the prospect of receiving more letters, Ace wrote back:

"I am as surprised to get a letter from you as to hear a tombstone speak. I don't want your army money. I want more letters. I never knew there was so much inside of you. God, Daniel, it's glorious. If you can still be in love from an army tent, I can do the impossible and be a poet in Chicago. And you're in love with somebody that is both impossible himself and hoplessly in love with you . . .

"You ask for news of him. Since you ask for it, I'll have to give it to you but it's bound to be all bad. Your Amos has sold his ass to a millionaire, but you know he did try to find work, he tried, but everything was stacked against him and so, to repeat, he has sold his ass to the rich. That's all the news I have from that quarter, but I'll go out and hunt for more if necessary in order to have your letters. I'll even black-mail to keep you in information. Amos is well taken care of, probably for the first time in his life, so you don't need to worry. Whether he will go on loving you or not, who knows. I hope he doesn't. You two could have been happy together until Armageddon, which is probably not far off, but you are a proud man and can evidently only declare yourself over the distance of our South. Maybe they will lynch you down there for your pride. Goodby and for God's sake keep sending the letters. ACE."

13

It was a full month after Amos Ratcliffe left Maureen's studio party that he finally made a collect long-distance phone call to the Masterson country house, Sampford Court. When Reuben answered, Amos asked him if he would drive to the bus station and meet him. Reuben, petulant and offended because he had not heard from Amos in all this time, at first snapped at him on the phone and then made it clear he would drive in at once.

The combination of Reuben's bad temper and immediate consent to meet him reassured Amos that the millionaire meant what he had said at Maureen's.

"Where the heck did you disappear to?" Reuben began at once when he faced Amos in the waiting-room of the bus depot. "And look at your new suit, will you, all out of press and mussed."

Amos hardly spoke in return. He was busy shelling and munching roasted peanuts, which he profferred to Reuben who testily refused them.

"Don't suppose you've had a decent meal in days," Reuben mused as he sat down beside the boy. "You promised me, Amos," Reuben began, stuttering slightly, "you'd call on me any time I was needed. What took you so long?" Suddenly he took hold of Amos's hand.

"Watch out what you do, Mr. Masterson, or I'll be picked up. Cops always on the lookout for dangerous degenerates like me."

"Oh be still," Reuben scoffed, missing Amos's sarcasm.

"What policeman would dare touch you when you're in *my* company?"

"Thanks for the lesson in class structure, Mr. Masterson," Amos said. "All right, *Reuben* then," he corrected himself at the latter's irritable protest. "I couldn't very well have showed myself in my new clothes to old Daniel, or he would have beat the tar out of me . . ."

At an eloquent look from Reuben, Amos stopped for a moment. "No, Reuben, I'll tell you straight: after Maureen's party, I felt I could never go back to Daniel, new clothes or no. I couldn't return to go on seeing someone I loved with my whole guts, and knew he would never let himself love me back . . . He really sent me to you that night at Maureen's . . . At the last, I hear he maybe changed his mind and decided at least to say goodbye to me. He came over to Maureen's—before he went to join the army, but we didn't connect . . . He went into service, I figure, to save himself the trouble of committing suicide . . ."

Reuben waited, silent, as if expecting more, then when it didn't come, said:

"When you disappeared those days, we all thought may be you'd followed after Daniel."

Amos could not control the angry tears which rolled now down his cheeks, and which he quickly brushed off with his hands. Reuben stealthily handed him a handkerchief, and Amos dried his face carefully with it and, at Masterson's silent insistence, since he had none of his own, kept it.

"You sure you didn't pay Daniel then to go off to the army, Reuben?" Amos made a stab at a joke, but his hurt suddenly returned in full force and he turned quickly away.

"Oh, Amos, I'm as sorry as I can be to see you caused

such pain . . . I know how much you cared for him. I don't know how he could run off and leave someone like you, frankly. . . . I'd have stayed for ever there just to be near you."

Amos returned slightly the pressure of Reuben's hand now.

"But, Amos, you must have known he was going back to the army!" Reuben cried suddenly. "Was your love affair then over, may I ask?"

"What love affair, Reuben?" Amos asked ferociously.

Unaccustomed to such strong feeling, it was Reuben's turn to look away.

"Don't tell me, Amos, if you don't want to," he said after a lengthy pause. "I don't ever want to pry. I have only one mission so far as you are concerned, to help you and to love you."

"I never had any love affair with Daniel Haws," Amos said with maniacal bitterness.

In a second-class hotel on La Salle Street, Amos allowed Reuben any and every liberty and intimacy. Indeed Reuben was surprised at the boy's sexual inexperience, for though Masterson himself had fewer sexual encounters than he boasted and most of these with the female sex, he suddenly felt deeply initiated and masculine before Amos, and his passion was increased by this fact. It was difficult for him to take in that Daniel and Amos's life together had been only "sleepwalking." Amos himself tried to explain, but at last gave up, admitting that he himself did not understand it.

After the first abatement of physical desire, Reuben lay back peacefully against Amos's body. He talked at such length about Daniel Haws that Amos, nonplussed, gazed at his new friend and said, "You sound more taken with him than you are with me."

"Daniel wasn't my type at all," Reuben pooh-poohed, "too masculine. But he was certainly the deeper of you two." He spoke hastily, then apologized for this remark when he saw it had stung Amos's pride. "Oh you're more of everything, Amos," he said. "All I meant by 'deeper' is that Daniel loved you more than either of us understand, else how explain the sleepwalking, and well, he gave you up to me through love, that's clear."

"Oh for Jesus Christ's sake, let up, Reuben!"

"Tell me where you've been all these past weeks," Reuben asked, bending over his conquest now, moistening the youth's curls with his mouth. He looked down at Amos's wreath of pubic hair which at that moment, catching the light, resembled an aureole. Leaning over, he kissed him again and again.

"Reuben, you wouldn't believe me if I was to tell you," Amos lay back languid under the cascade of Reuben's caresses. "Fact is that's the trouble with my life. When I tell people about it they think I'm lying. My life is odder than any pack of lies a maniac could give out."

"Supposing then you tell me the unbelievable truth."

"I went to the district, as Eustace still calls the colored part of town," Amos began. "See, some months ago, Ace was very keen on the occult and he even got Daniel to go over there with him to Luwana Edwards'. She's a spiritualist and fortune-teller. Has her own church now. She was awful taken with Ace, but shied away from Daniel for some reason. She told Ace he had second-sight. I wandered around after Maureen's party, into Washington Park, and then I thought of Luwana Edwards. After all I had to spend the night somewhere. But she told me too cheerfully she couldn't admit me even when I explained my situation and she also wanted me to know she didn't forecast the future any more for anybody . . ."

"And after Luwana's where did you go?" Reuben asked bitterly.

"After Luwana's?" Amos laughed. Then turning moody, he continued, "You know Luwana said something funny just before I left her place. She said she was aiming to pass her gift on to a friend. I think she meant Ace."

"You like colored people, don't you?" Reuben mumbled, abstractedly. "I can see how sick you are over Daniel's leaving, Amos," he went on. "It was wrong of me to make love to you, I guess, but I couldn't stop myself." He began covering Amos's body with hungry embraces. "Suddenly the unobtainable is ours," he said, and his eyes filled. "Do you think you can ever be serious about me, Rat?" He used the nickname with intrepid hesitancy. "I'm really in love with you, way over and above the physical. I'm head over heels."

Amos seemed a thousand miles away.

"You'll get over Daniel," Reuben went on doggedly. "After all, he ran out on you. Tell me you'll try to get over him! Listen to me, Amos, I want you to come out and live at my house. Mother's house, that is, but it's mine, too, after all."

"After all." Amos smiled and touched Reuben's hand gently. "Well, when do you want me to come?" he said wryly.

Reuben balked at the question, and walked about the room, dejectedly. Amos studied the body of the man who had just showered him with so much feeling. Despite his growing corpulence, Reuben was not unattractive, and in fact the scars on his chest and legs, from his war service, somehow added to his good looks, but whatever he had, it left Amos cold.

"I'm trying to get Mother ready for your visit," Masterson was saying. "I've told her as much as I can for the present about you and me."

"You mean you're trying to get *me* ready for her, Reuben," Amos spoke up, rubbing himself with a hand-towel. "Well, I'll never be ready. I don't belong anywhere. Can't even make it with niggers, Reuben. I'm just real enough for a sleepwalker to love, I guess. That's all Daniel could ever do too, so we were two of a kind. Sleepwalk to my bed and look at me like I was the new moon."

"So Ace told me." Reuben hung his head, ashamed perhaps he had discussed the matter with the poet. "Amos, what does it matter if Mother doesn't understand. Come anyhow. She'll accept you or she can lump it."

"I fell in love with my mother before I knew who she was," Amos began, as if alone. "My mother and I had an affair not too dissimilar from what we've been doing now."

"Oh for the Lord's sake," Reuben turned away from him. "Don't make a horrible joke of such things."

"You said I was honest and told the truth." Amos turned away from him also.

"While you were off with your colored people, I was slumming too." Reuben went back to the remark he had let slip earlier. "I spent a few minutes of time again with Ace Chisholm. What a fantastic character!"

Amos grimaced at Reuben's choice of words.

"He can't have been a good influence on you, Amos."

"Look, Reuben. You've got to get a few things straight for once and all . . . I don't have the luxury of choosing who is a good influence. I'm adrift in the sea, so I have to grasp whatever I can get hold of . . . Besides, who's to pay any attention to me but somebody like Ace? He admits he's a monster, at any rate."

Amos's eyes lingered now on the scars of Reuben's body.

"Do my war injuries disgust you?" Reuben inquired, somewhat piteously, but there was an undertone of anger, along with the hurt of rejection he had been suffering all night at the hands of Amos.

"They're the realest thing about you, Reuben. They make up for your fat tummy."

The older man blushed, then managed to get out, "Well, I'm glad you like something about me at least. Oh, I didn't earn my scars any more than I do my money. They came to me easy and got cured easy. I have Purple Hearts and the rest in my bureau drawer, but I'll be as honest as you are. I'm no hero, and if I were, you could make me feel I wasn't. I just love you, that's all there is to it, and I could drink your come in goblets . . . Unfortunately the feeling isn't reciprocal. You don't care for me at all, Amos."

"Yes, I do, Reuben. You're a good friend."

"If you could only love me a little bit as you loved him."

"Love Daniel! I'd like to kill Daniel. I'd like to barbecue his balls while the bugger is tied live to the stake. That's what I'd like. I could cut the bastard to ribbons."

"You love him, that's all you're saying. What I want to try to explain now is Mother. She's really my Grandmother. My mother and father both died when I was an infant. My wife died about two years ago—she'd been ill for so long, and my Grandmother—my Mother as I call her—has been nagging me to re-marry. I won't minimize the problem, Amos."

"I bet I'm in for a warm welcome from her then," Amos said.

"You've got to come with me, Amos. I can't live without

you, now there's been this between us. I don't know what it is that's happened. I don't know what you are. But you're everything for me. Have been ever since I set eyes on you at Daniel's that evening . . . And I could understand even then how somebody like Daniel, who isn't even queer, going off his rocker over you."

Amos covered his eyes.

"Amos," Reuben went on, scarcely conscious of what he said or indeed where he was, "you're larger than life. You came from a crossroads, Ace told me. He's wrong. You came straight from the hand of Creation . . . Let me tell you again—I could drink you in goblets." He let his head fall over Amos's sex.

"Yeah, you got the love bug for sure, Reuben." Amos lay back, his mouth slightly swollen under Reuben's kisses, a dazed lack of concentration in his eyes.

"You've got to come and live with me," Reuben now cried out. "Hang Mother. I'll die without this now. Tell me, Amos, you'll come."

Once he had calmed himself again, lighting a cigarette, Reuben inquired: "Do you know what Ace Chisholm advised me to do?"

"Cut my balls off, I suppose."

"He advised that if I couldn't make it with you, I should marry Maureen."

Amos scarcely seemed surprised, and this disappointed Reuben.

"You don't care what I do, do you, Amos?"

"Well, what do you want out of me, Reuben, outside of teaching me how to tremble in front of your matriarch?"

"I told you I wanted you."

"'Fraid you can't marry me, Reuben. And I don't think

your Mother-Grandmother would find me a fetching bride."

"Just tell me you'll come out there and live with me."

"I'll come, Reuben, I said I'd come. It's you keeps warning me I can't come maybe."

"And you'll stay with me always, promise?" Reuben held the boy to him so tightly it pained.

"I'll stay as long as it lasts," Amos told him.

Walking around the room now, Reuben gave off a kind of soliloquy. "Ace Chisholm can't speak without wounding one's sensibilities. He talks to me as if I were nobody, an idiot. My name and position mean nothing to him. In a way I like that. He's sincere that way. Have you heard the names he gives President Roosevelt? I never heard anybody called such names, not even by my black Republican relatives. He calls you a whore and worse, of course. Do you know what he said to Maureen, who laughed over it? He told her, 'Marry your queer millionaire. You'll be rich and he'll fill his house with boys from other men's stables. You'll be the wife of the queen, about as important as an eunuch in a harem. You'll be the fifth leg on a fine old chair. You'll turn to adultery and your millionaire faggot won't care, and he'll end up taking your conquests to bed with him . . . ' Yet he told Maureen it's the only marriage that is thinkable for her."

"Holy gee, you memorized it, Reuben!"

"Amos, Amos, come with me tonight. Do you hear?"

The boy nodded, and waited for the feel of Reuben's mouth on his flesh.

14

During the years Reuben had lived with his grandmother as a nonpaying guest in the thirty-room country American mansion overlooking Lake Michigan, safely isolated in the suburbs (he had moved in at her plea that the depression had more than halved their income, they must save on expenses, and furthermore she needed a man about the house), the old lady had chafed and fumed because he was not producing for them an heir. He, on the other hand, counted this period of time as his most carefree, almost his happiest, because his wife Letty's illness while enabling him to take advantage of the safe respectablity of being married and earning him the sympathy of all who knew him, permitted him at the same time to indulge in all the pleasures forbidden his married friends, without risk of outright criticism, especially his friendship with handsome young men.

While young Mrs. Masterson had lingered on, the old lady's constant cry was, "Why can't Letty go? Haven't we doctored enough!" and after her funeral, before she was hardly cold in the ground, she began with her new nagging, "When, Reuben, for God's sake will you marry and produce a grandson for me!"

Amos's coming therefore could only be regarded by her as a senseless and irritating postponement of her hopes and plans and a kind of deliberate dereliction of duty on Reuben's part.

The senior Mrs. Masterson's influence on Reuben was so incalculable that he never, in fact, began to be aware of its full extent. Obsessed as she had always been by money and social position, she drilled into her grandson from his baby-hood that he had a "name," that he belonged to a "front family," and that he would have to live up to it. It was name more than character that counted, and character, he deduced from her teaching, itself was subsumed under name, and from this idea he was never able to escape.

"So then we are to be made happy by the arrival of your young friend—what did you say his name was?" Mrs. Masterson suddenly opened the door on the crisis itself, with no attempt to disguise her loftiness and bitter lack of compliance.

"A good Saxon surname," she nodded on hearing Reuben repeat *Amos Ratcliffe*.

Having once been a poor girl herself before her marriage, the elder Mrs. Masterson not only detested poverty in others, but feared and distrusted the poor. Of course she had been the first to agree with Reuben, who had used her own line of reasoning, that those with name and position should help those who had neither. "The poor, my dear grandson," she never tired of pointing out, "are hardly ever worth the powder to blow them up with. But we can't allow them to stand milling about and breaking the plate-glass, can we?" In this one respect she agreed with the otherwise "deplorable" Roosevelts: crumbs can and shall keep back the ranks of the paupers.

One evening in March the meeting between the two important people in Reuben's life took place. As Amos came through the interminably long hall, accompanied by Reuben, on their way to the dining-room (Reuben had arrived as usual late), Mrs. Masterson, from her position at head of the table, was able to observe the boy approach. His undeniable good looks struck her immediately, but what held her eye even more was an undeniable something else, far beyond the "marks of poverty" which she expected in any case to see. She could only reflect in her astonishment that the boy advancing to meet her wore a look of expectation of unnamable horror.

She felt an irresistible wish to touch, even to pet the young man, and at the same time an overmastering urge to order him from the house. Yet had there been no Reuben at that moment—such was the strange confused tumult of feeling which came over her—she would have certainly made him her heir. Somewhat aghast at this unprecedented rush of impressions and feelings, Mrs. Masterson came to herself only when she heard Reuben's voice, impatient at having had to repeat himself several times (he mistook her failure to reply as due to her deafness).

"Well, you're late, even for you, my dear Reuben," the grandmother cried in her deep voice, starting from her own reverie. She permitted Reuben to kiss her on her cheek, and then, unaccountably, took Amos's hand before her grandson's own introduction, "Mother, this is young Mr. Ratcliffe about whom I've told you so much."

"Then, Reuben," she replied, not having taken her eyes off the boy, "I can see that as usual you've told me nothing at all."

"I suppose he is to be my albatross," Mrs. Masterson told Reuben, to his considerable astonishment, the morning after Amos's arrival at Sampford Court.

Reuben, who was waiting for the "long talk about everything" she had insisted on, jumped slightly on her choice of metaphor.

"For one thing," she went on at his look of surprise, "your Amos is capable of winning hearts . . . But there isn't time for him in my heart or yours, Reuben. Time's run out for both of us . . . We can't devote ourselves to charm and beauty. When they go or our hearts change, what do we have in their place?" She seemed to be speaking suddenly to herself.

Snatching some papers from her desk, she then discussed certain matters of business, a bad investment or two her "ass" broker had made for her, and then without warning she flew at the target again by shouting in the manner of a deaf person: "What in strictest fact do you know of him? Who were his parents, why is he through school at such an early age, and why should you be attracted to one so young, so entirely out of your circle, our circle, our way of life . . . Are you so desperate for companionship?" she could not keep down the note of alarm. "And why do you not *contemplate*, at least, marriage? I'm waiting for answers, Reuben!"

"As usual," Reuben sat down at the furthest end of the room, "you've asked me enough questions for us to be in conference for a month of Sundays."

"I have the time for it, if you do." She put down a heavy gold bracelet, which had come loose as she had waved her arm at him. She folded her ancient veined hands one over the other, and an immense stone on a middle finger shone fitfully in the morning light.

"Of course," she continued, "he is a charming boy, a personable boy. Good manners too. And I gather from the faces of the other guests he must have said some acceptable things while at table . . . He was sober too, while you were in your usual evening condition.

"But," she cried, interrupting him before he had time to utter a syllable in defense, "you can hardly have decided to fit your life around that of a boy with mere good looks who passes for clever at his studies."

"Let's say then I have, Mother."

"It's quite early in the morning for jokes."

"I am in dead earnest." Reuben rose and turned his back on her for a moment. The old lady sensed a new kind of strength in Reuben—this was not like his usual self.

"I had intended to take up the question of your drinking, but I see we'll be closeted entirely with the problem of Mr. Ratcliffe!"

"Mother, I'm crowding forty years of age, and I shall drink if I choose. . . . As to Amos, well, if you would prefer me to leave your home, I'm prepared to do so." He took the plunge. "But you said some years back, if you'll recall, that you needed me at Sampford Court. Very well, I'm willing to stay with you and be needed, if I may fetch out Amos here to be needed by me!"

"So we're to strike a bargain on that, are we?" she smiled. Something of her old small-town New England humor, Reuben supposed, came out then, but he was too out of sorts to be charmed or amused by it.

"What you're saying in effect then is that all you care for is your own happiness, if one can call a prolonged infatuation happiness, and to blue hell with your responsibility to your name and fortune!"

Reuben snorted at her burst of ire.

"Mother, I don't want to remarry, if that's the subject you're trying to force to discussion. And that's final. Besides, I don't care for women!"

"You told me you were very happy with Letty before she became an invalid."

"Oh that's all so long ago it seems it happened to another man. . . . I'm happier with Amos."

"Amos, whatever he is, is not a woman."

"That's why I like him."

"Yes, of course!" she cried, despair getting the better of her wrath. She tapped with her husband's riding whip, which she now employed to press the button for calling the servants. "Very well, Reuben. But why can't you hire him then as your valet or paid companion, instead of wining and dining him about town as if he was fresh down from Olympus, and drawing all eyes to you both. . . . He must cost you a pretty penny."

"As a matter of fact, Amos costs me less in a month than some of the tiresome Social Register women of your choice do in an hour."

"Certainly, Reuben, you know me better than to think I'd approve of a mere rich woman for your life . . . I'd approve of a girl of good family without a cent to her name, if she came along, and you know it. I even like that young person who paints, Miss O'Dell." Here, unaccountably, Mrs. Masterson laughed heartily.

"Well, why don't you bring Miss O'Dell to keep you company here, then," Reuben said, going along with her mood, "and allow me to keep Amos?"

"I'm too old to hear nonsense about great matters, and since you've brought up the matter of your age, so are you."

"I'm not going to give up Amos, for the simple reason I've found happiness with him."

Reuben rose to leave, but she gave him such a terrible glance he sat down again.

"He's a substitute then for a son, which you've never had!" she thundered.

"That's just what he is not!" Reuben roared back at her.

"Then I *don't* understand." Mrs. Masterson now stood up, sniffed her camphor bottle, settled her shawl more loosely about her neck, and stiffly changed chairs.

"Well, dear Mother, I don't intend to talk till understanding dawns on you: I value time nearly as much as you do, after all. But you've never tried to understand me. If you think I'm going to marry to follow your wishes, you're vastly mistaken. The world has been coming alive for me again, and if necessary I can get on without any money from you. If you prefer your Presbyterian circle and wish me out of the house, say so. It's you who've worried about the depression and expenses, and who spoke of loneliness and living only with servants, and so I moved in long ago, but if you've changed your tune and you don't dread any longer all the things that bothered you before I came down here, say so, and I'll depart."

Mrs. Masterson, to his considerable astonishment, broke down. The hand with the flashing stone covered her eyes, and she emitted heavy groans, the first emotion of such kind Reuben had ever seen her betray. It was the beginning of her fall.

He did not try to comfort her. "Well, Mother," he said severely when she had dried her tears.

"Reuben," she tried to regain her voice and composure, "if you need him that much, then of course you must do as you feel you must. As to leaving Sampford Court, that is out of the question. You shan't go a step. Of course I need you and of course you must stay . . . But," she was almost herself again, "as to your throwing money about, that must not occur. You have no money except in stocks that pay now poor, if any, dividends. It is I who control our fortune and will until I go, and you owe it to yourself and all of us, to the country, to stay here and keep down expenses. We're on the verge of some cataclysm, and we must stay together until the emergency is over. Thank God, you are too old to go to war this time, my dear boy."

Mrs. Masterson, an avid reader of history, was then off on

a discourse on the causes and consequences of the last "Great War" when Reuben, in a manner not usual with him, unceremoniously interrupted her:

"You've hinted about, Mother, that you'd like somewhat more information about Amos's background than you've felt I cared to give you. Actually I know next to nothing, but you'd best be informed he is an illegitimate child."

He stopped speaking then not so much to gauge the effect of his words as that suddenly the full weight of Amos's confession concerning his own mother, came to him now in all its blinding meaning for the first time, and struck him into silence.

Mrs. Masterson sat gazing at him, calm and unmoved, when he came out of his reflections.

"Amos calls his mother only Cousin Ida," Reuben stammered, blushing.

"You may rest assured," he heard his grandmother's voice, "that if you think I am going to conduct an inquisition on the poor boy, you show very little insight into, or appreciation of, my character or methods. I'm surprised at you, Reuben. I bid you good morning . . ."

Reuben stood indecisive before her, but made no movement toward the door. She had already turned away from him to the papers on her desk, but looking up from her work after a bit, almost accidentally, and finding him still in her presence, she found it impossible not to add:

"My heart aches for you, Reuben. I wish you didn't care so for this boy."

The tears came to his eyes, and humiliatingly enough for him, she saw them, but there was now neither a look of reproach nor pity in her expression, and she accepted the kiss he bestowed on her cheek by pressing his hand briefly.

15

"What, may I ask, are you reading this time at table?" Mrs. Masterson addressed Amos one chilly April evening when the two of them had sat down together again, without other company, at dinner.

Amos handed her the Greek text of Xenophon's *Banquet* and allowed the old lady to satisfy her curiosity by leafing through a few of the pages. Quickly returning the book, she explained that she could now only stumble through her Greek, and shot a glance of troubled admiration at the boy. She had noted steady changes in him since his arrival, not so much owing to his now sizeable wardrobe, whose costliness made her wince, as perhaps because of his new regimen, daily baths, regular meals and uninterrupted slumber. She could only wonder if Cousin Ida herself would now recognize her son.

They owed their present strange communion with each other to a change no less startling in her grandson's habits. Shortly after Amos's coming, as if relieved by the unexpected fulfilment of his hopes, Reuben had begun absenting himself every few days, often staying overnight in town on one pretext or another. Left thus alone, Amos and Mrs. Masterson found it difficult, if not impossible, sometimes to hit on topics for conversation which would carry them through the meal. She quizzed him on his upbringing in Southern Illinois, for this topic genuinely interested her, but Amos's pained reticence prevented her from going into it deeply, and finally, in resignation, she had allowed him to bring his book to the dining-room and even read as she talked interminably in his direction, while the servants whispered.

As for Reuben, once he felt reasonably certain Amos would not "run out" on him—after all Sampford Court was some 40 miles from Chicago—his absences became more frequent and he made no pretence of hiding what he went to the city to do. As Amos pointed out in a bitter letter to Eustace, "I've become the child Reuben Masterson had to give birth to, and it's no surprise therefore he's deposited me with his Grandmother, while the heir and father goes scot-free to worship Bacchus."

Many a cold spring evening, and spring was very cold that year, the old lady and the transformed Amos sat together through dinner and the interminable evening, guarded and attended by the formidable staff of servants, fed like royal prisoners and bored to death by each other's company.

Mrs. Masterson went to bed around nine and lay the rest of the night in a kind of wrestling match with Morpheus, never really falling sound sleep until three or four in the morning, that is if she heard Reuben's footsteps returning from another of his evenings out.

The day after looking at Amos's Greek book Mrs. Masterson had sent her butler to a bookstore in town, to procure a complete English translation of Xenophon's *Banquet*. It took him hours and several phone calls to the university Greek faculty, to locate one. She wondered whether her reading of the dialogue helped her to grasp, at least partially, the goings-on that then occurred in her house.

Galled by Reuben's neglect and wearied with the interminably long evenings, Amos had a diabolical inspiration. He remembered the Swedish gardener, whose principal task was to keep the rooms of the great house supplied with flowers from his nursery. Recently a widower, he lived alone in servants quarters a short distance down the ravine, and his appearance was striking enough that Amos felt he would have graced a banquet at which Socrates was a guest more becomingly than aristocratic Reuben himself.

In the middle of the night, disturbing Mrs. Masterson, who took the boy's exiting steps for those of her grandson's return from carousing, Amos, an Indian bathrobe thrown over his pure silk scarlet pajamas, carefully adjusting his usual nocturnal erection, walked confidently to the Swede's cottage, whistling a little tune. At the door, he knocked loudly and waited, still whistling. The gardener finally heard the whistle, if not the knocking, and admitted his guest through sheer astonishment. Once inside, Amos had no intention of leaving again, for he had got chilled through and through from the raw air, and the sight of Boötes rising in the east had made his teeth chatter.

When Reuben did not answer her imperious "Is that finally you?", Mrs. Masterson rose, threw a quilt about her shoulders, and opened the door of her grandson's bedroom. Surprised at the absence of both Reuben and his favorite, and feeling now suddenly a bit light-headed, she sat down at Amos's desk. Her eyes fell on a half-finished letter the boy had written to Cousin Ida; under this letter lay a handful of others, opened, and thumbprinted by his reading, bearing an indecipherable Illinois postmark with the sender's name, Ida Henstridge. Mrs. Masterson struggled with her conscience only briefly, then she read avidly not only Amos's unfinished epistle, but with even more rapt attention all those Cousin Ida had written her son. The small town speech, like a current of warm air, brought her immediately back to long-forgotten thoughts and feelings and relationships before her marriage.

She read of Cousin Ida blaming herself, defending herself, and at last crying out against Amos's unjust bitterness, and accusations against his "lot." Cousin Ida begged him to have patience, trust, hope, to thank his benefactors, even though he could not stand the rich, as exemplified at any rate by Reuben and the "old lady of the castle." She begged Amos to put up with the shows of wealth now as he had with poverty and going without and to remember he was a man and that meant he could be free. "I would give anything sometimes if I had been born a man, for then I would not have to sit here and wonder where my next dollar was coming from, but on the other hand, I would not be the mother of a fine son like you, and that makes up for all the rest, dearest Amos."

She told then how Aunt Lily had come by the other day, and she and Ida had told the tea leaves to see what lay in store for Amos, and then they had got down together on the rag rug in the kitchen and prayed that things would go better for him in the future. "But if they don't, dear Amos, come home, remember the Welcome sign is always out." There were other details, the canary had died, and she wouldn't get another, but would leave the cage in its old place; Widow Martin down the alley had taken away her membership in the church because of her disliking the new preacher's wife; the refinery was being sued by the town for its failure to control the suffocating fumes and bad odors it let loose. "I am glad," she concluded, "Mr. Masterson shows you such strong affection and interest, for there never is any word from your father, and I wonder, Amos, if maybe he isn't dead."

Having read all the letters, Mrs. Masterson sat on, feeling a terrible weakness and foreboding and sudden extreme giddiness. She desperately hoped Reuben might come in, for she felt too weak to call out for the servants. Then her eye fell on a slender sheaf of pages over which was scrawled "Visits from a Sleepwalker." She read, uninterrruptedly absorbed, for an hour more.

Still yawning in huge paroxysms, the Swedish gardner Sven studied his late caller. His command of English being negligible, and a man of few words in his own tongue, he took off his thick slippers, and curled up beside his self-invited visitor. He recognized Amos as the guest of Mr. Masterson and in his bewildered way decided that owing to an influx of guests at the great house either the old lady or Master Reuben himself had sent the boy to ease the overflow.

After the light was extinguished, he was soon put to a different view of matters at the floodgate of affection which Amos, stung by his having lost Daniel Haws and being shut up away from everything in the country, poured out on the taciturn gardener, whose own arms deprived of love by his wife's death yielded too easily.

After the first appeasement of feeling, the gardener was bold enough to ask why Amos's feet were so hard and horny, for he could not help comparing them to his wife's, whose toes had been like cotton when pressed against him. Amos explained that he was an inveterate walker from his earliest childhood in the country and had spent most of his time in Chicago on the streets, exploring every inch of the city afoot. At this the gardener, with a certain uneasy superstitious dread in his voice, asked if the boy would show him his feet.

Amos willingly obliged, and placed his toes on a white rug that lay by the bed. The gardener, who slept naked, covered himself against the cold with Amos's borrowed bathrobe, and studied the boy's feet under a lamp.

"Goat feet you have!" he told Amos. "And the rest of you so handsome!"

The gardener looked up from his kneeling posture.

"What's swinging between your legs?" Amos chided.

"The devil scolds where he's to blame!" Sven cried. Puzzled from the time he had opened the door on his caller, he shook his head now half-pleased, half-dismayed.

"Does your master know you have such goat-like feet?" Sven inquired.

"I have no master but me," Amos snapped.

The Swede was walking into the next room when Amos cried with a kind of wistful alarm: "You're not going off now like everybody else?"

"Oh no, no," the gardener smiled, "you'll see what I'm about, and you'll be glad."

Amos could hear him drawing water, and he returned with a heavy tray containing a silver wash basin, a bar of freshly opened soap, a thick brush, some cloths, and talcum powder. Without more ado, he plunged Amos's feet into the basin, and began washing them vigorously.

Moved by such ceremony, Rat mumbled appreciation and studied the gardener's face. He was about thirty, and health and an open honesty of expression gave him appeal, and besides his biceps bulged like turkey eggs.

"You have walked to the ends of the earth." The gardener looked up from his task from time to time. "Only the devil has walked further."

During the bathing of his feet by Sven, Amos as was his habit whistled rather loudly, and this familiar whistle was heard now by Reuben Masterson, as reeling from his night

on the north side of Chicago, he started up the path to the
big house. He stopped short in his tracks, inspecting his
breath as it issued into the air. The whistle came again, this
time unmistakenly from the gardener's cottage.

Wheeling about suddenly, grinning with anticipation of
seeing Amos, and not suspecting anything out of the ordi-
nary, Reuben knocked at the door of the cottage calling
Amos by name.

"Don't answer," Amos begged Sven.

"But I must," the gardener showed no sense of the danger.

"It'll be bad to let him in, I'm warning you."

But Sven with his old-world respect for authority and
proper behavior, was already on the way down, without having remembered in his haste that he still had on the bathrobe Amos had worn rather than his own.

"What are you doing with my robe on?" Reuben stammered on confronting the Swede in the doorway.

"Your young friend is here," the gardener replied.

Having caught sight of Amos naked on the bed, Reuben
picked up a rawhide whip from the wall and struck the gardener with it full in the face. Tasting blood which ran copi-
ously into his mouth, the Swede almost involuntarily
knocked his employer's son to the floor. Amos, in a rush of
spontaneous enthusiasm, clapped his hands.

"You applaud, you rotten little bugger, when it was I
who took you off the streets and gave you your first decent
living!" Masterson turned his fury on the boy, scarcely noticing that the gardener had bent over and lifted him up off
the floor.

"I applaud this fellow only because he returned an insult
like a man, not out of ingratitude for your incredible gener-

osity to me." Amos found himself speaking in the style of
Xenophon as translated by himself.

"Get out the both of you!" Reuben cried, mopping the
blood from his face with the handkerchief handed him by
the Swede. "A fine plot you've been hatching behind our
back!"

"You won't dismiss me, sir," Sven began to Amos's incredible disgust. "You can't turn me out, Mr. Masterson,
for something I did not mean!"

Reuben smiled. "Maybe your young bedfellow here will
intercede for you."

"Please, please," the Swede looked from Amos to Reuben, imploring, and gave every evidence he was about to
kneel there before them when Amos suddenly struck the
gardener a vivid blow.

"Where are your balls you were so proud of a few minutes ago?" the boy bellowed, while Reuben turned suddenly
hysterical and began to sob.

"You're too young to know what being without work is,"
the Swede turned to Amos bitterly. "If you've walked the
streets, I've walked them more!"

"Get packed, and we'll clear out." Amos spoke with cool
imperiousness.

The gardener shrugged his shoulders in hopeless agreement. Then, removing the Masterson bathrobe, he laid it
gently on the table. Reuben sat there too stupefied to say a
thing, but looking up just then, whether brought to by the
sight of the gardener stripped, or realizing that having fired
an employe of whom Mrs. Masterson was so inordinately
fond and proud would bring him trouble from that quarter,
he suddenly stood up and asked Sven to forget everything
he had said and to stay.

"I've been overhasty, Sven," Reuben said, finding it very difficult to speak to a man standing stark naked in front of him. "Besides," he finished, "I've no right to dismiss you. That is Grandmother's province. After all, I'm hardly more than a lodger here myself."

"No, no, I'll leave, sir." The gardener turned away confused. But then pointing to Amos, he cried, "Why did he have to come here, sir, and put me to this test!"

Both men suddenly gave Amos the same indescribable look as if they had discovered at last the common source of their trouble and torment.

"Is there a drop of spirits in the house?" Reuben inquired, and in a way of conciliation he threw the bathrobe around the Swede's shoulders. "I think, Sven, we could all stand with a stiff drink of something."

Sven brought out a bottle of brandy, a gift from Mrs. Masterson, who allowed liquor in the homes of her servants on the understanding it was to be used only in cases of illness or exposure. It was, as Reuben found out hardly to his surprise when he tasted it, third-rate. When the gardener could not find glasses, Masterson, despite Sven's bashful reluctance, insisted they drink out of the mouth of the bottle.

Amos declined to join them. He sat on an old buffalo rug in the center of the room, and glowered. After a while Sven, prompted by Reuben, ceased even to wipe the mouth of the bottle and the two men, becoming mellow, exchanged confidences. They railed at boys like Amos who preyed on widowers, and devoted a great deal of time to repeating pledges to one another never to tell "Lady" Masterson the events of this night. Reuben then assured Sven that he could stay at Sampford Court till hell froze over. He was in the midst of a long speech of effusive congratulations on the gardener's physique, poise, and gentlemanly bearing, together with a panegyric on the glory of having Viking ancestry, when Amos rose in disgust and, throwing the ill-omened bathrobe over him, opened the door.

There to his astonishment stood on the threshold old Mrs. Masterson, garbed only in her dressing-gown, her hair in long yellowish white braids falling over her shoulder. Her gaze went immediately from Amos to Reuben, with his arm around the stark naked Sven. Both men were in violent sexual excitement. She turned her look of icy outrage and blame to Amos and her lips moved to say something to him, but a convulsion of some violent kind came over her, and she lurched forward to fall at the boy's feet.

Reuben rushed forward. "Mother, mother!" his hysteria mounted.

"Tell him to leave me, my only son!" The old woman continued to fix her attention on Amos. Her jaw hung down from the effect of the stroke she had just suffered, and only her eyes, out of her entire countenance, kept their former expression. "Can't my death have some decorum?"

Reuben looked accusingly at Amos, as if it was the boy who had both drawn the grandmother to the cottage and who had been responsible for her fall, but Amos gave him back so fierce and eloquent a look that Reuben turned away.

Sven, hastily clothed, now carried the old lady to a large overstuffed easy chair. She closed her eyes briefly only to open them wide on Amos, who glowered at her in rapt attention from the shadow of the open door.

"Hasn't this chosen Satan of yours any shame?" she cried. "Can't you pay him to leave, Reuben, if he won't depart peaceably? Make my last moments decent, for God's sweet sake, even though your own life is foul!"

"Please go, Rat," Reuben entreated, deadly pale.

Amos wheeled about in the direction of the mansion.

A few minutes later, carrying a small grip, he was on the main highway to Chicago.

16

"Coming, coming!" Carla Chisholm, exasperated, cried in response to the rain of peremptory blows on the door to the apartment. She put down the jar of night cream, and wiped off her chin and throat with a tissue.

To her considerable astonishment, on lifting the safety lock, she found herself facing not Ace, whom she had been expecting for hours, but a stranger. Even had she known the heir of Sampford Court (she had scarcely set eyes on him before), she probably would not have been able to recognize Reuben Masterson in his present condition: he was bleeding from the nose, wore two great blue bruises over one eye, his collar and tie were torn; only his tweed suit and benign expression hinted he might be "somebody."

He identified himself, and she stood aside, still speechless, to let him come in. Recovered from her initial shock, and thrilled to know who it was, she invited him to sit down and managed to make him feel more comfortable, more quickly, than any other woman he had ever met: she brought him a half dozen things from her medicine cabinet, and most soothing of all, a fifth of Weller bourbon, which he opened immediately.

Between constant probing of his mouth to see if he had lost teeth, he summarized his news: Amos had run away and Mother Masterson despite the fact she had had a stroke, had given permission to "fetch the boy back," which he was here to do. Next Reuben explained, with a bit more detail, the reasons for his own condition. He had driven into town in hopes of finding out Amos's whereabouts from Eustace, had parked nearby, and within seconds after locking the door of the car had been set upon by "roughs" who had knocked him down, but had left without robbing him, scared off by his cries for help.

During his perfunctory recital Reuben looked about the apartment anxiously as if searching for traces of Amos's presence.

"Amos isn't far off," Carla reassured him. "He's gone with my husband over to South Parkway to see some Negro spiritualist they have the habit of calling on every so often."

Reuben looked at her in a dazed manner and she wondered if he had heard her.

"Mr. Masterson, why don't you spend the night here now? We've an extra place as Clayton Harms has left us."

"Please call me Reuben," he said. "Well, if Amos will be back, I'll gladly wait forever." He could not completely suppress his tears.

In wishing perhaps to divert him from weeping, she chose to discuss Clayton Harms at length. She helped herself, at the same time, at his invitation, from her own bottle of bourbon.

"We've been through an upheaval nearly as terrible as what you've been through with Amos and your Grandmother and the gardener. Perhaps as terrible, for us." She considered the whole affair. "I don't know whether you ever met Clayton Harms." She explained quickly her own running away with another man, and Clayton's moving in and taking over in her stead.

Wiping his eyes with her tissue from his own grief, Reuben listened now more through stupefaction than interest.

"Clayton asked Eustace to choose between us almost from the first day of my return. One day in a rage he threw four of five of his electric signs out of the window, nearly killing some people, and demanded a final say-so, but none of us could give one. Then a few nights ago, we had this knock-down-drag-out fight. God, it was awful. Ace and he beat one another to a pulp, and Clayton turned on me with a bread knife just before the police got here." She pointed to a few inconclusive scratches on her arm. "But Reuben dear,"—she shot a glance of sympathy at him—"here I am chatterboxing away when your grandmother is at the point of death! Forgive me."

"I think Mother—I always call grandmother Mother," Reuben came out of his reverie, dry-eyed now, "I think she plans to die in order to show me how much she disapproves of my present life and Amos. She has the will to do so."

"Aren't you exaggerating a bit because of your present depression?" Carla was taken aback in spite of herself.

"That's just what I'm not doing, dear lady," he said huffily. "She'll die to make the rest of my life a lasting lesson from her to me."

He rose and applied a menthol stick to his forehead. "Where, by the way," his bad temper continued, "did you say Eustace took Amos this evening?"

"They went to Luwana Edwards, a Negro spiritualist. But in regard to your other remark I think, if you don't mind my saying so, it's all the other way around, Reuben. Amos took Eustace. I think Amos can lead him by the nose any time he takes the notion to!"

"Are Eustace and Amos that way with one another? I mean lovers," Reuben brought out rather quickly.

"No," Mrs. Chisholm sighed deeply, "they're not lovers

at all. It might be better if they were for this way they both try to exert power over one another, and that's what makes their relationship so dangerous. Each eggs the other on to do terrible things."

Reuben groaned, offered the bottle of bourbon to Carla, who refused it, and then he went on with a serious narration of "everything": all that had happened after the night at the Swedish gardener's. Mrs. Masterson received Sven's full "confession" as to what had occurred, including the washing of the boy's feet. In the end she forgave the Swede (he had thrown himself on his knees several times), and since he was almost as good a Lutheran as she was a Presbyterian, they all, including Reuben, knelt down at the last in prayer in the den. She kept Reuben behind, after Sven's departure, to go over and over the "ceremony" of the gardener's washing the boy's feet. She claimed she could not get it out of her mind, and then a few hours later, while in a state of high good spirits, she had suffered an additional stroke.

Carla again pressed her invitation on Reuben to spend the night. He could have her bed, and she would be glad of this excuse to sleep with her husband on the davenport in the front room. Finally, more than half drunk, Reuben kissed Carla, told her she was a charming attractive kid, and stumbled into her bed, where he was immediately dead to the world, while Carla sat on waiting for her husband to return from Luwana Edwards's.

Reuben Masterson, in Carla's bed, had been dreaming he was conversing with Cousin Ida. He saw the hollyhocks, just as Amos had described them, the tar-covered gravel alley leading down to the river, and in the big backyard, flanked by a line of catalpas, Ida herself, hanging up her clothes on the line and threatening the robins if they came near her sheets. Catching sight of Reuben, she advanced in his direction, took the clothespin out of her mouth, called him by name. Facing him, only inches from his face, she whispered to him her fears: Amos, a poor swimmer, had gone to the quarry and not returned, and would he, she wondered, go down there and see if anything was amiss.

Waking, Reuben found Eustace Chisholm sitting on the bed beside him, studying him. It was just light outside.

"Go on back to sleep, Mr. Masterson," Eustace spoke. "I only wanted to be sure it was you . . . Thought Carla maybe had made a mistake about who was sleeping in here," he added under his breath.

Masterson gave a pleasant good morning, extended his hand, which Eustace ignored or did not see, and then cried: "Is Amos with you?"

Eustace shook his head.

"Do you know where he might be?"

"Who are you to ask?" Eustace rose from the bed, then looking down at the floor-boards said, more civilly, "I don't know where he is."

Reuben pulled on his shorts, and bending over began drawing on his shoes. Red-faced, he looked up to inquire, "I don't suppose by any chance you remember where you left him?"

"In Washington Park, for your information," Eustace snapped. "At 2:30 A.M."

In the kitchen, paring his nails and cuticles with a knife, Ace mumbled in ill-temper:

"You and Amos come at a time when I don't have any further use for you." He looked in the direction of the newspaper scribbled over with his poems. "I'm on Daniel Haws now full-time, with generous helpings from Cousin Ida's letters . . ."

Reuben started on hearing each name, and Ace stopped speaking for a moment to observe him carefully.

"I make a rather fair pancake for breakfast, Mr. Masterson." Eustace had put down his knife, and was observing his guest narrowly.

"I don't want to inconvenience you," Reuben began.

"Oh come out of your make-believe, sir." Eustace was already beating the eggs and milk together. "Just to be alive means inconveniencing everybody around."

Reuben sniggered.

Cooking the pancakes, Ace went on: "I'm not surprised you jumped so when I mentioned Daniel Haws's name. After all you robbed him of Amos . . . But when I say I'm on Daniel, I mean he's writing me two and three letters a week from Biloxi, Mississippi, with special-delivery on Sunday, and I'm soaking all he tells me right up and pouring it right back into those" (he nodded in the direction of the defaced newspapers).

"I'm afraid I'm not very interested in poor Haws," Reuben said morosely, as Eustace set his platter of steaming pancakes before him, with a jar of maple syrup.

Reuben began eating the cakes dispiritedly, then perked up a bit, and complimented his host on the flavor.

After finishing the pancakes, and after having had his question answered as to the whereabouts of Carla—she had gone to work in the "tin mines"—Reuben asked cautiously:

"I suppose you think a man of my age pretty silly being so badly in love with a boy."

"Are you?" Eustace snapped.

No match against Ace's cutting manner, Reuben nonetheless went on: "Everything is Amos with me now. You'd be doing me an awful favor if you'd take me to him, or at least tell me where he stays."

Eustace shrugged.

"I take it then he doesn't want to see me again." Reuben studied the poet's face attentively.

A look of such despair gradually came over Masterson's face that Ace spoke up then, in spite of himself:

"He doesn't want to go back and live with your Mother, Reuben, sure enough."

"Please tell me where he is."

Eustace got up and looked out the window overlooking the alley to watch the everlasting unloading of meat for the delicatessen.

Biting his lip like a traitor, he said, "By and by I'll give you where he lives."

"Mother's dying so that's no reason now for him to keep away."

"I believe maybe you are in love." Ace stood with his back now to the window, watching Reuben absentmindedly. Making a clicking sound with his tongue, he went into the toilet and peed loudly into the bowl, washed his hands, dried his fingers on his long black hair, came back, and sat down on the floor and began playing klondike.

He heard Reuben breathing heavily and irregularly and in consequence he kept his eyes averted from him and fixed on the playing cards.

"Yes, siree," Ace said cheerfully against the painful silence. "Everybody shows up here with their problems. This is the clearing house for busted dreams."

"Would you believe me if I told you I'd never been in love before like this," Reuben spoke with difficulty. The note of supplication and hopelessness in the older man's voice was so grave that Ace looked up in spite of himself.

Astonished at the look on Reuben's face, Eustace swallowed, finally got out: "Maybe . . . But why don't you look at it like this then. It won't last, and you'll be free of him."

Reuben flailed under the scrutiny the poet now gave him.

"I'm trying to visualize you as a doughboy in the trenches." Eustace smiled after a bit. "I think I can see how you looked . . . Embraceable, if not adorable."

Suddenly Ace scrambled all the cards up, gathered them all together and put them away in the box.

"You don't even know who Amos is," Ace frowned, rising. "Not that it has much to do with love, I suppose. I only *just* know, but you don't at all . . . Daniel Haws got wind of it though, and skiddooed, I judge, on that account. But you—. Come on in the front room where we can lounge more."

A dirty orange sunlight was coming through the latticed blinds in the room, and a searchlight shaft of scintillating dust particles crossed over the threadbare hooked carpet. Ace sat down on the made-up davenport, which had been his and Carla's bed last night.

Touching the article of furniture he sat on, Eustace mused: "You accomplished one thing anyhow, Reuben. By taking her bed, you let my wife sleep with me for the first time in better than a year."

Masterson stammered a minute, then got out, "Wouldn't Clayton Harms's leaving have done that in any case?"

Eustace blinked and then managed a grin.

"I almost wish you hadn't told me you'd left Amos in Washington Park, and at the hour when you did leave him," Reuben spoke out of breath. He shaded his eyes with the palm of his hand on which some precious stone flickered faintly.

"Some men are immune to evil customs," Ace droned. "Maybe that immunity is what Amos and Daniel had in common. That's why they loved one another, and always will, even though they no more than touched here . . . Take Amos, he looks frail, small bones, small beautiful skull, eyes like forget-me-nots, but he's hardier than you and me combined. Since Daniel left, he's given his ass to black and white without stint or refusal. If he has a charmed life from danger, it's because he's already fatal. A strong man would have died . . . No, Amos was ruined a long age ago, in his mother's body . . ."

Walking up and down as he did when alone, Eustace continued: "He blames it all on a July afternoon in a small-town soda-parlor where sitting in an ice-cream chair his runaway Dad give him the short sword on the cervix . . . But don't you know that story?"

"You know damned well I don't," Reuben spoke with heat.

"His runaway Dad," Eustace went on, ignoring his own rhetorical question and Reuben's anger, "got to thinking about him about fifteen years after he had left his knocked-up girl friend who goes now under the name of Cousin Ida."

As if he had been there, and seen it all with his own eyes, Eustace related the following narrative:

Dad drove up in a Franklin touring-car, vintage 1913, with side-curtains, running-board, funny spokes in wheels, and a statue radiator-cap. He parked up on the lawn of Ida's ramshackle house camouflaged by hollyhocks, dwarf sunflowers, morning glories, and wild plum trees. Little sea shells bloomed in the garden, frilled snowy curtains hung behind the tiny windows, notes to the milkman stood in bottles on the back steps, clothes lines swayed, birds galore hopped about in the lettuce, mint and sweetpeas, and there that beautiful boy lived, a bastard brought up more lovingly than an heir. The runaway Dad began walking up to the back door, stopped, probably to let them see who it was.

He's a six-foot four gent, who couldn't make an honest day's living if he was put in a chain gang, had been in jail for passing bad checks four or five times, all bone and sinew, cocked sailor straw hat with black ribbon, faroff blue eyes like his son's, not fixed on life, a yearning mouth. He rapped at the back door, standing by the milk bottles, and the woman he had got in the family way fifteen years before looks through the screen, and damned if she didn't recognize him.

"Ida, is the boy to home?"

"What boy are you talking about?" she replied. "You no-account sonofabitch." But there Amos sat having his coffee out of a deep saucer.

"Does he drink his coffee out of a saucer like a infant?" his father grinned.

"He drinks it any way he wants to drink it in my house, specially since it's out of my sweat and toil he has growed up to this age."

Hat in hand, Amos's Dad did not budge, said he knew he had no rights, but asked to be able to take the boy out for an hour's spin. After permission was wormed out of her, the Dad drove Amos to this out-of-the-way ice-cream parlor near the state line, a favorite stop for truck drivers hauling smuggled merchandise, ladies committing adultery with local building and loan directors, where a preacher was shot to death by a widow who was losing his love, where the local fairies used to come late afternoons.

After the soda-jerker had served Amos, his Dad, not having ordered anything for himself, dry-mouthed, morose, observed: "You eat your chocolate nut sundae more like a girl than a boy." Pushing aside his dish, Amos turned linen white, waited a few seconds, wiped his lips free of syrup with his own fresh-laundered handkerchief.

"I could be a girl for all you know," Amos declared. He stood up and pushed the chair hard against the table.

"Sit down when I tell you to!" His Dad flushed beet red.

"Go back and put your condoms on the line to dry," Amos spoke loud enough for the few other customers to hear.

"You sit back down here, you God-damned little snot," his Dad cried, eyes smarting, gasping for breath. "Nobody speaks to Cy Ratcliffe like that . . ."

At a sudden movement of his father's fists, Amos seized a water glass, smashed it and ground the splintered edge into his father's arm, and pausing only long enough to observe blood staining the torn sleeve and the cry of anguished surprise, the boy went cooly out the front door of the soda parlor.

Amos walked the ten miles back to town, taking the long detour around the stone quarry, beyond the river. Later he claimed he could not remember a single step of the hike back to Cousin Ida's, but he must have tripped and fallen frequently for his face and clothing were stained with earth, grass and vegetation.

"What did that big stiff do to you that you're in this condition?" Ida cried, stupefied, opening the door on him.

"If you ask me that again, I'll kill you, Cousin Ida," Amos warned her.

Seems always about that time of the year, the Ku Klux Klan, not a strictly nigger-burning outfit in that town but more a combination of odd left-over law-enforcement chores and a fraternal get-together group, holds some kind of pow-wow by the charred wreckage of the old First Baptist Church that was blown to smithereens some years back killing seventeen robed members. The way to the burned-out church cuts across the gravel road and the big cornfield beside Cousin Ida's house, on the outskirts of town. The processions of the Klan, announced more by clouds of white ascending dust from the crushed stone than by any sound or confusion, always filled both Amos and Ida with vague concern and uncertain terror. In the not too distant past, when Ida had been summoned into the Mayor's office on a charge of serving liquor to her boarders without a license, she had called the annual parades to the attention of the Mayor, a prematurely white-haired fun-loving sport who had made passes at her before he was elected to office. He had promised to look into the matter, but of course never did.

Hours after he had stabbed his father, Amos, sick in bed with a fever, had smelled the dust from the road and heard the crunch of the marcher's footsteps. Terrified herself that the two events, the stabbing of Cy and the parade of the Klan might be connected (Amos's father was low-down enough, she knew, to wear a sheet), Ida put out all the lights in the house and shut the storm door tight.

"You keep under the covers and stay in bed no matter what happens here tonight," she told Amos.

The procession haltingly got past the house on its way to the church; she sat by his bed, and suddenly touched his forehead: his scalp and hair were wringing wet, his teeth clicking like dice in the box.

"I have a very impressionable boy on my hands." She echoed under her breath her old speech to the Mayor. "The damned Klan has no right to march by my house in their robes and scare us to death . . ."

After a silence, Ida spoke directly to Amos: "If you're

moanin' about what you done to your Dad, you can quit, for I called the county infirmary. I'm sorry to tell you you didn't do him no real harm and he was released with only eighteen stitches . . ."

Then taking real concern at the cold sweat that oozed over all his body, she crept into bed with him, hugging and comforting him with words and caresses. Along about two o'clock they heard the last of the marchers coming home from the pow-wow, and when everything was dead still again, this thing happened.

"Amos already told me, Eustace, so please stop . . . for pity's sake." Reuben tried to put some force into his voice, and then turned his face to the wall.

"Amos had kissed her," Ace went on. "At the relief she had felt over the procession finally moving away, Ida had lain back hardly aware of his lovemaking and then in sudden terror of realization she had whispered, 'Amos, not your own Mother, for God's own sake!' "

"It was right after that," Eustace concluded, "that Amos came to Chicago and into our arms . . ."

They listened then to the sound of the key being turned and the door's almost human squeak, and Carla's high-heeled step, meaning the work-day was over. Suddenly, under her metallic "Anybody to home?" they caught Amos's soft querulous tones. He had returned.

17

According to friends, Eustace Chisholm showed signs of going rapidly down-hill about the time Reuben drove Amos
out to the Make-Believe Dance Hall, off South Parkway,
though Ace himself put it down to his last visit to Luwana
Edwards, the colored psychic. He claimed she had given
him a funny look and he hadn't felt right afterwards. By
"going down-hill" the friends meant he had given up nearly
any little interest that remained in his poem and seemed to
want to hear about only two subjects, Daniel Haws in Mississippi, and Amos Ratcliffe in Chicago and environs. (He
thought of the two subjects, however, as one.) He was also,
some people claimed, losing his memory.

If anybody had asked Eustace which of the chapters in
the life of young Rat he liked the best (though he would
have considered this a literary question, to be treated with
contempt) he would have had to reply, "The Make-Believe
Dance Hall."

The death and funeral of Mrs. Masterson had been acted
out, so to speak, in advance by Amos and Reuben that
night at the Make-Believe Dance Hall, and it was perhaps
his sense of ceremony and ritual—considerably deranged
though it now was—that had permitted Reuben to go to
such a place at such a time.

Eustace tried to hold in memory for as long a while
afterwards as he could, the sound of Amos's drawling honey-
like yet steady male voice as he chronicled the final episode
of his life with Reuben Masterson.

He did not get the whole of the story from Amos alone,

he got parts of it in scraps of conversation from others, like Maureen O'Dell and Reuben himself. But he always remembered it in Amos's voice and accent.

Driving Amos into Chicago, Reuben had tried to be philosophical and summarized the failure of their relationship.

"Don't you require kindness, Amos? You don't seem to. Don't you require love? I had so much of that to give you. All my life I've wanted to love somebody, and I never could find anybody to pour it out to. My wife was unloving, didn't like anything about love. All she required was a formal drawing-room patter and etiquette. She liked to have me hand her in and out of cars, peck her on the cheek, arrange her orchid. And now I realize that all my life it was only men I could have loved after all, when I guess it's too late . . . But I loved you more than anyone I ever met before. I could have been happy with you for life, had you allowed me to love you . . ."

"Happy with you and Grandmother?" Amos glared at Reuben.

"You have the most piercing eyes I've ever seen. If they were black instead of blue they would kill, I suppose. One can almost see your brain when you stare so . . ."

"The eye is an exposed part of the brain," Amos snapped.

"There, you've spoiled that for me, too," Reuben groaned. "You who are so beautiful don't want beauty."

"Not the Oscar Wilde kind," Amos said. "I don't know what I want."

"Then you'd better find out, my very dear, very young man . . ."

Amos guffawed.

"Well, you never found out what you wanted, Reubie, and you had twenty or is it two hundred million dollars behind you to have a go at discovery. Guess that's what's wrong with you, all dough and no character. You were tutored to do everything. I'm surprised your Grandma didn't have you tutored to fuck, or teach you herself out of her Old Testament . . ."

Reuben stared gloomily ahead at the twin shaft from his headlights on the dark curve of road.

"Frankly, Amos," he said, after swallowing his anger, "you remain a deep mystery to me. You come out of that far south section of Illinois, you're part hill-billy and yet the most sophisticated keen person I think I've met . . ."

Amos adjusted the folds of his scrotum with deliberate ostentation.

"You believe in nothing, I guess," Reuben droned on. "You're hard, and I guess that's what Mother senses in you."

"She sensed a rival in me, Reubie." The boy spoke with a trace of his old heat.

"I don't understand what you mean."

Amos grunted. "Your grandmother never wanted anybody to love you. She never loved you, and she couldn't have stood it if anybody else ever came along to show her how she couldn't. She never loved anybody. That's how you got so gummed up. And are you gummed! Without your money to keep you mucilaged together, man, you'd be in worse shape and condition than me. I'm such a mess I can operate. That's an achievement, I warrant . . ."

"So Mother never loved me," Reuben smiled, as if pleased he was at last a serious topic of discussion.

"You're in her bag for life, Reubie, and when they bury her, they will bury a lot of you with her. That's why you're right to go dancing tonight. It'll be a beacon of hope for the rest of your life. 'I went dancing the evening that Grandma was dying,' you can tell your descendants, if any."

"I should let you out of the car," Reuben said, deathly pale.

"It may save what little life's left in you, Reubie, going to the Make-Believe Dance Hall."

Whether you call it the Globe City Ball Room, which is the name that greets you outside in pink letters (its original structure had been a car barn) or, with the fairies, the Make-Believe Dance Hall, it was only within its precincts, Reuben claimed later, that he had ever been forgetful of the passage of time. He could have gone on dancing there forever.

When they had entered, Amos looked up to see the big orange-colored globe fixed in the middle of the high ceiling. The sole source of illumination, it might have been the greatgrandaddy of all the paper moons that ever shone. It seemed crowded inside, with a queer odor like that given off by crushed moths or butterflies, yet as a matter of fact there were few people in attendance by crowd standards; perhaps it looked full to Reuben and Amos because they were the only whites.

They were immediately popular, Reuben felt, the moment they entered the door, though he wondered later if it was perhaps Amos's looks and the impression he himself gave of bulging with silver and reserved favors. The black waltzers and fox-trotters were ready to go again at the sight of the two whites, despite an already long evening behind them with Terpsichore (it was just 2:00 A.M.) Everybody stopped dancing for a moment when they entered and then the two were asked as partners, and there under the orange moon, they went at it until each was so weary he could only rest his head on the shoulders of the partner of the moment in motionless embrace.

"You said there would be no girls here!" Reuben came up to Amos between numbers, complaint in his voice as he pointed to some dancers in skirts in the far corner of the ballroom.

"Them—girls?" Amos smiled. "Don't you know that each of those crepe de Chine dresses you see covers a writhing eel?"

Just the same Reuben wished to dance only with the boys who wore pants, he said he felt he had done with dresses. "Thank you for this, Amos!" Reuben cried, going off with a new partner. "I'll thank you for the rest of my life."

Suddenly Amos saw in the middle of the dance floor the dreadful familiar face of Beaufort Vance, the abortion doctor. He must have recognized Amos at almost the exact moment, for turning his glance away from the boy, he disappeared into the crowd. Amos looked about to see if by chance Clark B. Peebles, Vance's assistant, was also present, but he was nowhere in evidence.

Then it got less and less crowded, and the clock ticked on toward daybreak.

The sight of the abortion doctor and the feeling of the approach of day dampened the little enthusiasm Amos had for the ballroom in the first place, and he retired to a table near a heavy velvet curtain from which with sardonic amusement he could watch Reuben, whirling and giddy, throwing himself from partner to partner.

The passage of time had by now become indistinct to Amos. Looking up suddenly, he saw there was nobody dancing any longer in the ballroom and the ten-piece orchestra had vanished, except for the piano player who was tying his shoe-string. When Amos looked down, he saw that Reuben was now lying on the floor beside him, a satisfied grin on his lips.

"There's nothing like the bare floor to straighten a man out, Reubie," Amos mumbled. "I hear that's why the Mexican peons are so beautiful. Sleep on flat old terra firma, a few swipes of straw under their ass. Of course I've slept on flat ground a good many thousand nights alongside Cousin Ida, but that ain't why people say I'm beautiful . . ."

Amos hummed the blues number he had heard earlier:

> I left my Mother,
> Why can't I leave you?

Dozing off again, he had some sort of hazy dream about Beaufort Vance and Clark B. Peebles and, awakening, found Reuben's fingers stretched out in sleep around his ankle.

"Your light is out." He placed his toe on Reuben's hair, and saw that the older man was still under. "You get drunk just like a baby. I can't get drunk, Reubie. Know that? My heart just won't be slowed down I guess for anybody except old Bugger Man Death . . . As to love, Reubie, I'd love you, sweetheart, if I felt you were for real for more than a split second. But you're an American baby. Your Grandma knows what's what about you. To think you were a doughboy, and wounded, with a bureau drawer crammed with medals. Yet I feel I got to protect you. Your Grandma thinks I've brought you down in the world. Fact is, maybe I've brought you into the world. A man is lucky when it takes only four drinks to knock him out. You've been asleep all your life, snoozing in the gray maw of money and when you're awake, you're in partial anaesthetic. Still even *you* suffer . . ."

Amos rose, looked in vain for the piano player, and began

two-stepping with some imaginary partner under the extinguished orange globe.

"I could be any man's son," he called to all the empty tables and chairs. He slipped and fell to the floor.

Hours later, from his sprawling position on the sawdust, he saw Reuben listening to his wristwatch and checking it to see if it could be so late.

"Christ Jesus, what have I done?" he heard Reuben's excited falsetto. "Why didn't you call me? What have you let me do?" Reuben cried. He was beside himself, and Amos understood that he would be blamed for having taken Reuben away from his dutiful vigil at his grandmother's deathbed.

They had trouble getting out of the ballroom. The door had been locked on them, and Amos gave a display of his strength by breaking it open. A fine rain was beginning to fall as they drove up the driveway of Sampford Court, where an immense ornate funeral-parlor limousine was parked, waiting to take Mrs. Masterson's body to the undertaker's. She had died shortly after Reuben had left for the ballroom.

Reuben sat there in front of the steering wheel, blubbering.

"You allowed me to kill Mother," he accused Amos again and again.

III

under earth's deepest stream

18

In his letters Daniel Haws, who in "life" (by which he meant civilian life) had been morose, taciturn, bitterly reserved and almost inarticulate, poured out everything. He did not even hesitate to touch on the master passion of his existence—Amos. The letters to Eustace arrived now almost daily.

Eustace Chisholm's appetite for other people's mail may have had its genesis in the frequency with which he haunted the city streets. Unlike small towns, cities contain transient persons without fixed abodes who carry their letters about with them carelessly, either losing them or throwing them away. Most passers-by would not bother to stoop down and pick up such a letter because they would assume there would be nothing in the contents to interest or detain them. This was not true of Eustace. He pored over found letters whose messages were not meant for him. To him they were treasures that spoke fully. Paradise to Eustace might have been reading the love-letters of every writer, no matter how inconsequential or even illiterate, who had written a *real* one. What made the pursuit exciting was to come on that rare thing: the authentic, naked, unconcealed voice of love.

It was also true that people had always written *to* Eus-

tace. Few people may have respected him deeply (Daniel
Haws hardly did), but nobody had contempt for him
either. They probably wrote to him for the reason that he
was interested, had the time and capacity to listen, would
not judge them, and did not feel infallible. If Ace offered
any advice, he did so in the way of a half-suggestion, which
he was the first to admit might be incorrect. Everything in
his own life may have been a failure, but he never tired of
listening to others or reading their mail. What Eustace had
not bargained for was that Daniel Haws was to prove both
his supreme reward and his nemesis in the matter of letters.

One stifling summer morning Ace was curled up on his
davenport reading the latest from D. Haws, when without
so much as a rap of his knuckles, Amos Ratcliffe walked in.
Mrs. Masterson was dead, of course, but Amos had made
no effort to return to Sampford Court. As Ace put it, the
same old people had him on their hands.

"Is that a letter from who I think it is?" Amos asked,
sitting down on the floor near Ace's feet. Ace nodded.

" 'There is this Captain Stadger,' " he went on reading
aloud now from the part of Daniel's letter where he had
been interrupted. " 'Don't like the looks of him a-tall, not a-
tall. Claims he seen me in the regular army before this Roosevelt emergency. Chicken shit on that. He keeps at me,
though. Says he knows I got Indian blood. Named the
tribe, too, Cherokee, as he claims he's an expert on blood
strain. Always hanging around watching me. Says if I don't
do just right he'll send me to a really tough outfit, and that
will make me appreciate how good he is to me here. It's
taken me a long time, Eus, even to learn how to salute
down here. Showing respect for bastards so low-down on
the evolutionary scale makes my gorge rise. Mostly every-

body down here are all little pissy Southerners. Can't see sometimes how I'll last, and then again I never want this emergency to end. 1 got to last. I got to get through the army, for Christ, I could never come back to Chicago, and where else could I go, answer me that. I'm in a real ghost world down here, Biloxi, Mississippi, Spanish moss hanging from trees, we're in tents, snakes galore, though mostly harmless, this funny little city on the Gulf, with its nigger town out of bounds. But everywhere I go, in the swamp, or by the ocean, or in the woods, there's Captain Stadger always to bump into . . .' "

"Give me that letter."

"You go straight to hell," Ace replied.

"I deserve those letters, you stingy bastard, more than you do." Amos made a kind of whimpering sound as he spoke which gave Ace pause.

"If I'd give you one of these letters even to look at, you'd be apt to put it right in your mouth and swallow it, I'd never get it back, that's sure. And I'm going to hold on to them."

"Going to put them in your newspaper poem, I reckon . . ."

Ace showed impatience to get on with reading Daniel's letter to him, but Amos interrupted again with: "Does Daniel ever ask about me?"

"Oh, I guess once in a blue moon."

"And do you give him news of me?" Amos spoke almost bashfully, not able to disguise his eagerness.

"Well," Ace studied the boy. "I told him about the scandal you caused at old lady Masterson's funeral." The poet rolled his tongue about in his cheek.

"I bet you dressed that story up good and proper."

"No, I told it just the way I heard it, without embellishment. How the funeral parlor director had not known you and Mr. Reuben Masterson were in front of the casket making love, and when he pressed the electric button for the curtain to go up which separated the bier from the audience of waiting mourners, there you two were both drunk and necking, Reuben's hand on your open fly for the whole world to get the picture . . . I added that as a result of that scene the heir to two hundred million had been read out of the Social Register and was about to leave Chicago . . ."

Amos hung his head, but couldn't control a wry grin.

"You never know a party until he writes you a letter," Ace mused, intoning. "Take your ex-lover, Daniel Haws. When he was here, all I ever got from you or him about yourselves was next to nothing. Then he gets epistolary, and by God, I've got him full-bodied. See all of him. He's epic, he's great, he gives me everything on PX stationery."

Ace, however, did not immediately go on with the reading, and Amos took his turn to say: "Remember all those wonderful nigger love letters I found in Washington Park that day and brought right up here to you, quick as I could hot-foot it? You grabbed the whole damned packet, never said thank you, kiss-my-foot, and you got at least four chapters for your poem out of them. And remember those murder threats I found near the corner of Woodlawn and 67th Street, brought 'em to you before I'd half-read them, and here you won't even give me a peek at the letters of the one person matters to me in this beat-up life of mine."

"Calm down, honeybunch," Ace snapped. "Matters to you! Nobody matters to you, and you know it. You're still mad Daniel Haws didn't go to bed with you, that's all. Had he done so, you'd have treated him like dirt. He must have sensed it, and that's why he left you . . . I don't know what's going to happen to him in the army, but it couldn't be much worse than had he shared his life with you . . ."

"*Talk about the chicken-hawk,*" Daniel Haws's letter continued. "*That's Captain Stadger. You must know how a hawk acts, Eus, you was in the country once. He's waiting to get something on me, and have me red-handed. Admitted as much himself. Dogs me when I'm on KP, bobs up from nowhere when I go to town. Other day stopped me when by accident I drunk out of a Lister bag that was in the colored section of our camp here. 'Daniel, you like to drink after niggers?' he inquired. 'Answer that question. A real American Indian like you want to drink out of a nigger's Lister bag?' I had to apologize for an hour and a half, salute my hand off, and all the time he is not looking at my face, he is gazing around me, as if he thought he might spy me wearing side-arms. Looking at some part of my body that he can't seem to find.*

"Why is it, in my life, somebody is always hounding and devilling me. Take my mother. After my father died in a coal miner's riot and I took his place in the pits, at the age of 13 sole support of her and my kid brothers and sisters, she hounded me from sunup to sundown; when she died and the kids were placed in homes, I went to live with this M.D., drove for him, niggered for him, he hounded me morning noon and night; in my jobs in Chicago I always got the fellow in charge who knew how to hound; Amos hounded me, Maureen O'Dell, Reuben Masterson, all hounded me. I bet if I lived near or around you, Ace, I would bring it out in you too. But now I got the prince of*

*hounders, Captain Stadger, and he looks at me as if he's
been waiting for me all his life, and that he knowed I was
born to be hounded.*

*"One last word about this captain before I close. I never
felt the goose-pimples so hard as when I see him. Something is going to go wrong, and I've got to get all my
strength together, I can see, just to keep standing in the
same position. I got to get out of this man's army with a
clean bill of health. I can't leave it under any cloud . . ."*

Amos had gone back to his room on Dorchester Avenue
which he was sharing with somebody—Eustace was not
sure just who it was at the moment (Reuben looked in on
him occasionally to see he was not starving to death)—and
Ace sat on in the glowering Chicago twilight, a feeling of
strange malaise stirring vaguely inside him somewhere, as if
suddenly he saw the whole U.S.A. nothing but Daniels and
Amoses whispering and muttering to him in the falling
darkness.

For one thing, Eustace had taken a good look at Amos's
palm this afternoon, not having studied it for many weeks,
and he had caught a glimpse of a line in it that was new,
and that had brought out the hard goose-pimples on his
body also.

In his disturbance, Ace reached back to take up the tied
packet of old letters from Daniel, and began reading one
from weeks ago:

"Remember when Amos, or maybe it was you, dragged
me to a nigger fortune-teller named Luwana Edwards? She
wouldn't see me; she had already told your and Amos's fortune, but every time I went over to South Parkway and
stood at her big old glass door, she either wouldn't come
out at all, or would say, 'Huh-huh, no siree!' 'Why not,

Luwana?' I would answer her back. 'Am sick in bed,' she said. 'Stepped in some glass on the bathroom floor and got me a case of blood-poison. Can't tell nobody's fortune.' I knew that was made up, but I kept at her because I wanted to know about myself, and finally she let me have her reason: she seen a streak of bad luck for me, Ace, such as she had never in all her years of prophesying and forecasting witnessed before."

Without lighting the floor-lamp, waiting in the dark for Carla, Eustace thought about Luwana Edwards. In fact right after she had refused to tell Daniel Haws's fortune, she changed her name and gave up her profession. He had cast a bad shadow on her, his own luck was so bad.

"I saw worse than the Kingdom of Death on that young man's brow and hand," he could hear the voice of the Negro psychic coming to him. "I shook when I seen the signs, Mister Chisholm. My hands trembled, my knees turned to water, I done went into the house after closing the front door on him and kneeled before the picture of the Savior, and I cried till my heart would break. Does the world have to be so very violent and sad, precious Master? I prayed. Does the sorrow have to come in such wide-mouthed vessels for us to drink, Lord?"

She had knelt in prayer a long time, then, suddenly free, she had the word: she was released forever from prophecy and foretelling, she would give up the profane art of fortune-telling and devote her psychic abilities to her own Grace Evangelical Missionary Church.

But it was Daniel Haws's brow and hand which had effected her conversion and change.

19

Nobody had been sure why the Ku Klux Klan had burned a cross in front of Mr. Bates's cornfield behind the First Baptist Church that night in April, but later, months later, an official of the Klan had telephoned Cousin Ida and told her to quit her worrying, they had not had the burning on account of anything she might have done but because of one of the Jamaican blacks who was getting too familiar with a white parlormaid in old man Graber's house, a stone's throw from Ida's. But it was the cross burning in the Spring air that had caused all the trouble between her and Amos and had made him leave town and had deprived her of the comfort and support of a son who was now, she was certain, lost forever to her.

Ida's letters to Eustace arrived now more frequently (she had written to him ever since Amos had first mentioned Ace, in his first weeks in Chicago) especially now since Amos himself had quit keeping in touch with her.

But the letters to and from Eustace were not enough for her, and she felt, though she was only thirty-eight, that she was going down "the shady side" of life's road, without news of a son who was the paramount, yes, the only thing in her life. Of late she had had nothing but one terrible dream about him after another, and her pillow was wet in the morning from both weeping and the sweat of terror and anxiety.

She had frequently called Lily over to have a talk with her about it, and once a few weeks back when she had started to tell Lily the story of that April evening and the

Klan, Lily had said firmly, "Ida, I don't think you'd best finish what you've started to say. Not for my sake, precious, but for your own. Don't tell me. Certain secrets a woman must keep buried in her own heart. This is one of them. We have to carry some things with us to the grave, and hope the Lord will turn away from judging us for them, and judge us only on the ones we can talk about in daylight."

When therefore Cousin Ida had sent Lily a new urgent summons to come down to the end of the road for a "serious talk," Lily was afraid that Ida was going to broach again the unwelcome subject of what had happened between mother and son.

Lily entered the house with a tight mouth, as if to say, "If you so much as open your mouth again about that matter, I'll never darken this door again. I've been your best friend, but there's a limit to what friendship can endure."

Lily sat down stiffly and refused Ida's offer of a piece of fresh-made cinnamon cake.

"Something awful has happened or is about to happen to Amos." Cousin Ida went to her worry without preamble, placed the Woolworth sheet of stationery she had just received from Eustace Chisholm, and which contained the exact sentence she had uttered, in front of the music teacher. "Lily, for God's sake, read what Mr. Chisholm has wrote."

Lily refused to touch the stationery for several long seconds. Finally she took it.

"What on earth is wrong with you today, Lily? You act like I had the bubonic plague! If I can't turn to you in trouble," and her emphasis of the word trouble brought back to both women Cousin Ida's role a number of years ago when she had gotten Dr. Sherman Stokes to perform an illegal operation for Lily when pregnancy would have ruined her

career as a music teacher in a small town. Dr. Stokes, a respected M.D., had only done it because he was so fond of
Ida.

"All right," Lily said, remembering the old favor. "Let
me read this gentleman's letter."

She read then.

"I think it's wonderful you don't have to use glasses, Lily,
when you use your eyes so much in your teaching," Ida ram-
bled on while her friend perused the letter, and waiting, she
took a bite out of her own cinnamon coffee cake.

Cousin Ida saw with impatience that Lily had now gone
back to reread what Eustace had written. Impatient, she
smoothed down her pretty home-made gingham apron with
the forget-me-not pattern, and looked pridefully about at
her immaculate kitchen.

Suddenly Ida noted with astonished surprise a look of relief, if not outright pleasure, spreading over Lily's face as
she read.

"What in God's name is making you look so glad with a
letter like that!" Ida could no longer contain herself.

She suddenly snatched the letter paper out of Lily's
hands.

"Ida, how unlike you, dearest!"

"Don't Mr. Chisholm's and my concern mean anything
to you?" Ida thundered, and rising, forgetful, the empty
cake plate fell from her lap and broke into pieces on the
floor.

Lily stooped down with her and helped her pick up the
fragments, uttering regrets.

"Ida, my angel, may I explain what you mistook for gladness in my expression? I thought the letter was going to
contain something much worse than it did! After all, it's

only premonitions so far, on this Mr. Chisholm's and your part . . . Not fact!"

Ida burst into tears in Lily's arms.

"I love you, Ida, and you'll never know how much. You're the dearest girl in the world. Your only trouble is you love too much. You're too full of love for your own good."

The two women sat then talking and reasoning things out. Then Lily tasted the cinnamon coffee cake.

"I wish you'd move in here with me," Ida said dispiritedly.

"Oh, the piano playing would drive you crazy, precious," Lily replied. "I can hardly stand it myself any more."

"And you think Amos will get through Chicago all right then and come back to us?" Ida spoke as if to herself.

Lily hesitated. There was the remembrance of the pack of cards, when at Ida's insistence, over a year ago, she had told mother and son's fortune.

She thought back to her own recollections of the boy. There was something about Rat, something she had never been able to explain, from the day when she had unsuccessfully given him a few piano lessons, then told him to stick to his Greek . . .

"We'll hear from Amos, in the world," Lily said ambiguously. "I'm sure of that." But Ida was not listening to her.

20

"The army is not going to be a Mother to you, but your dark bridegroom." Eustace had written this as a beginning sentence in a letter to Daniel Haws. For a long time Daniel was unable to reply to this particular letter. Like many things Eustace wrote or said, the sentence had an obscure but smarting meaning which struck home long after it was made. The words, "dark bridegroom," stuck in Daniel's mind as though it were the pain from a hot cinder cutting into his eyeball.

You are in the arms of the dark bridegroom, the Army.

Captain Stadger followed Daniel Haws about almost in the manner of a special detective assigned to him, manacled to his prisoner. Once Daniel looked down at his wrist as if to check whether there was a fetter resting there. The captain singled him out with his eye for observation in drill, in such duties as the cleaning of the officers' barracks, and elsewhere about the camp. He seemed always and invariably to appear after chow to watch the soldier go through the cleaning of his mess kit. After eating, Daniel had hardly risen from the grass with his empty kit, striking a soiled fork against the tin plate, than the captain appeared as from behind nowhere to watch him. Daniel began the ceremony of cleaning, putting the mess kit and its utensils in the dirty suds contained by the first huge garbage pail set on a bank of flames, then into the second garbage pail with its hot clearer water, and finally in the third and last pail which contained violently bubbling scalding clear water. Going up to the soldier, the captain took the kit and utensils out of his hand, inspecting, pressing the texture of the metal with his massive thumb and fingers as if to test whether it would bend. "See that sandpile," he ordered Haws. "Get your ass over there and scour this hardware till it shines like Jesus."

Blinking unaccountably, Daniel did not move. The captain grasped him by the shoulder, and although he seemingly exerted no force, Haws felt as if some central fiber and principal connection of bone had come loose from its anchoring within his body.

Sitting near the sand, scrubbing the kit again and again, only to have Captain Stadger refuse to admit it was clean enough, Daniel scoured on, but the place on his body where the captain had seized him ached out of all proportion to the second in which the officer had exerted his force on him. A fearful vision of Amos suddenly flashed across Daniel's line of vision, as if the face of the boy was reflected into the gleaming burning oval of his mess kit. Again Eustace Chisholm's phrase for the army echoed in his brain and formed itself on his mouth. Suddenly nauseated, he vomited near Captain Stadger's brilliantly shined shoes, saw them withdrawn quickly, then heard the officer's voice somewhere over him:

"Wipe your mouth clean of that puke, Private Haws, and then get on with your scouring . . ."

On his army bunk at night under the Spanish moss hanging from the live oak trees, Daniel Haws wiped his mouth again and again from some imagined stain, and thought back to when he had worked in the Herrin, Illinois coal mines. He did not remember childhood, he remembered only being little and called young, in the confusion of his family's economic distress, and going down the shaft, and bringing home his pay to his mother.

Daniel Haws once heard his mother say to a neighbor woman, "Daniel is the kind of a lad nobody ever thought to give a nickname to." That was the only time he had heard her describe him, outside of the day when he handed her his first pay-check and she had said, "*Son*," nothing more.

By the time his younger brother was old enough to go into the pits, Daniel had run off. He lied about his age, claiming to be older, and enlisted in the U. S. Army. His mother received letters from army bases all over the country, first the little towns in Illinois, then south in the Carolinas, Louisiana, and at last Nicaragua. But the army pay proved too pitiful to help her and her brood, and when he was just two months short of seventeen, he went over the hill. For a while, nothing was heard of him. Having never given the army his correct name or home town, the fugitive felt in time he could return to Herrin, Illinois, and went back to work in the coal mines. Then followed the ferocious strike of the miners and the bloodshed. The brother who had taken his place was killed, his mother died, and in a house chilled by death and hunger, he gathered together his younger brothers and sisters and told them they must break up, he could no longer keep the family as a unit, they would have to scatter and go and live with relatives. It took another year, however, to place them. This was the depths of the economic burnout (as Eustace Chisholm called it) and nobody—friend, relative, church, or Salvation Army—could find enough to feed another mouth without a lot of searching and complaining.

"Finally, I lit out," Daniel wrote Eustace Chisholm from the PX, explaining his life in one of those long letters composed on army stationery to the tune of *Amapola* and the

clink of crushed ice in Coca-Cola glasses. "I lit out for Chicago, in a box car on the Illinois Central . . ."

But Daniel had at least been free then—free to lie in alleys, sleep on doorsteps or elevated trains, free to panhandle,
sink, die, but free.

Now with Captain Stadger he was already in death's
kingdom. He knew that he would never get out of the captain's hands unless he allowed him to take some part of his
body as the price of severance, as a wild animal will dis-
member its own leg from the trap to go loose. He knew
from the first time he saw Captain Stadger watching him,
as though he had seen him years ago in some ancient dream,
that he would have to surrender part of his flesh to escape or
go down forever in the realm the captain ruled.

Then he caught malaria. They sent him to a hospital in
Hattiesburg, Mississippi. He was released before the medics
agreed he was cured, on orders of Captain Stadger who insisted the soldier be sent back "pronto" to his headquarters.

Daniel was writing his letter to Eustace Chisholm with
the fever still in his blood. Droplets of sweat, forming on
his brow, splattered rhythmically to the paper, while a terrible dryness and parching of the mouth and throat made
only a few more words possible of complete formation.

"Amos Ratcliffe has told you the story of his life, now
here I am telling you the story of mine," he wrote. "I only
heard Amos's full story through you, Ace, but I don't think
Amos ever heard mine."

"He didn't need a *story* from you," Eustace muttered as
he read Daniel's letter. "He needed—." He got up and
went over to the alley window and watched the Negroes
unload the kosher meat.

"Do the rabbis know which niggers unload their blessed meat?" he mumbled. "I wonder if they do."

He sat down again.

Eustace Chisholm felt unnaturally depressed. It was Daniel's letters, he decided. No, it was the face of the President and his wife smiling and telling everyone to be cheerful and give up fear. No, it was the feeling of the something we all carry in the marrow of our bones. No cheerfulness, no joy from wine or drugs can fully eradicate the ache of terror that resides in the marrow of the bones.

Looking at the photo of the President pinned to his wallpaper, Eustace mumbled on to himself aloud: "One thing Government will never be able to do, stop us from dying. Everything else they can *make* us perform, even killing one another. All our Presidents are killers, but they can't stop us from dying when the day for us to die comes. It's a good thing Dame Nature thought up death after the mistake of inventing life, otherwise we'd all go on being forever under some immortal captain or other in timeless slavery."

The man who had nothing better to do than watch black men deliver rabbi-inspected meat in an alley was "hooked" as much as Daniel Haws had been "hooked" in Chicago on Amos Ratcliffe. Eustace Chisholm was hooked on Daniel Haws's story as told in letters, and was a goner. The poet had been fascinated by little Rat, but he was taken over by D. Haws.

"I've got a sickness may not have a name," Daniel Haws had written. "I'm sick to the very bottom of me. I hurt everywhere. Inside, I'm all hurt, and have ever been. I've got a sickness which may have a name, and if it does, why name it to me? I won't remember it anyhow. Could you say, Ace, I'm boy-sick? If you want to call it that, I'd have half-admitted it in Chicago, but my sickness is so big now I couldn't feel any name would be right to contain it. Boy-sick, me that's mounted all them whores. I'm a whore's delight. Yet I'm boy-sick, Eus, if you want to say so. I'm lying here still under the same Spanish moss, it's not my country. My sickness, though, didn't come from being down here, it didn't come from the long hours in the mines or me being husband-son to my Ma. I must have come into this world with this hanging over my head, Eus: I was meant to love Amos Ratcliffe, without ever being a boy-lover, and that was written down in my hand. That's why that nigger woman wouldn't tell me my fortune. She said, 'I stepped in some glass and am in awful pain. Can't tell your fortune, sir . . . Not next week neither. I'm goin' away, besides.' 'Can't you ever tell it?' I inquired. 'Come back in a year maybe,' she replied. 'Doubt I'll still be around here by then.' 'That's right, I can see travel around you, will tell you that much,' she closed her eyes. 'Lots of travel. It will do you good.' "

Captain Stadger was looking for more evidence than sleepwalking had given him, and he didn't have to look long. The evidence he had been seeking, however, was not one half so good as some he came up with completely out of the blue. He had put his soldier on KP just about every day that month, for Haws's misdemeanors since he got malaria came to be legion: he had not made his bed properly, left peanut shells on his pillow, torn the mosquito bar, had not shined his dress shoes properly, dirty collar, buttons not polished on his O.D. blouse. But the unexpected evidence which the captain had never dreamed would turn up (he was going to have to manufacture it) came just after retreat

one hot July day about the time Amos Ratcliffe had returned to Chicago, following Mrs. Masterson's funeral service.

Captain Stadger, not finding things to his liking in Daniel Haws's tent, asked the private to empty out the contents
of his barracks bag.

Obedient in the same unhesitating way as when he had
responded to the imperious command of dismissal after he
had sleepwalked that first night, Daniel patiently unfas-
tened the neck of the bag. Out fell clothing, a package of
rubbers, letters tied with string, math books, some chewing
tobacco, and then, unaccountably perhaps to both of the
men, as if it were alive, falling at the feet of Captain
Stadger, a photograph of Amos Ratcliffe. The captain
stooped, picked it up, interrupting Daniel's quick flurry to
seize the picture, held it in both hands, studied it decisively,
pokerfaced.

Daniel Haws went pale and extended his arms defen-
sively as if he heard a row of rifles crack over his head.

"Ever notice how everybody down here talks like a nigger
except you and me, Private Haws?" Captain Stadger began carefully tucking the photograph into his crisp pants
pocket. "You and me talk more like mountaineers, I suppose. Some might even say moonshiners . . . We talk
alike anyhow, that's for sure . . . Don't we?" the captain
raised his voice ever so slightly.

Daniel Haws nodded, and stood stiff at attention.

"Now supposin'," the officer said thoughtfully, "after I
walk out of this here tent," and he looked down at his
wristwatch giving it the same stare of accusatory suspicion
he gave to men, "and after I am gone five, six minutes, say,
you begin to walking slowly after me, and catch up with me

in the O.D.'s tent, which will be vacant then except for us . . ."

He looked critically at Daniel's tie, the soldier straightened it with nervous fingers, saluted.

A few minutes later Daniel stood at attention, his hands firmly alongside the crease in his trousers, before the captain seated at his desk in the O.D's tent. Daniel aimlessly tried to recall what Amos Ratcliffe had talked like since the officer had mentioned the speech of mountaineers and moonshiners, and he felt in dimming memory that the sounds Amos had spoken must be also like his and of course therefore—as it had been explained to him—like Captain Stadger's.

"This photograph," the officer spoke sleepily, and then stopped. Daniel looked at the captain's hand to see whether he was holding the snapshot in question, but he was not.

"This boy whose photograph you have kept in your possession," Stadger began again, but at the sudden unexpected sound which came out, uncontrollable, from the private's chest and throat and which he may have thought was a disturbance coming from outside, Captain Stadger peered through the flap in the tent. Then satisfied that the sound had actually proceeded from the soldier, pleased, he resumed the question. "This photograph you kept so carefully is of course a member of your family, I suppose a younger brother . . ."

"No, sir."

The captain stared to show careful incredulity, surprise.

"Who then should be so unusually honored by you, Haws?"

Whether Daniel had lost track of time, or his fever had increased at that moment and he had missed words, he didn't know, but the next thing he saw was the open furious mouth and lifted tongue of the officer, the jugular vein distended improbably, demanding answer, and Haws heard his own voice say:

"Amos Ratcliffe, sir, a boy I knew in Chicago."

"A casual relationship or distant friendship you'd call it?" The captain became as quickly cool and collected as he had been previously savage and angry.

"You could call it so, sir," Daniel now stumbled, having lost his way.

"Or would you call it a special relationship and very close deep friendship, do you suppose?" the captain prompted.

Daniel sought mute permission to wipe the sweat that was gathering in a sheet over his brow and eyes, but his appeal was not recognized.

"The fact that you would honor a casual friend by keeping a photo doesn't seem very convincing or probable." The captain had begun what was probably intended to be a series of carefully constructed questions when the irrevocable words, along with a sudden rain of perspiration, came from the soldier in sounds like the snapping of a huge sheet of ice broken by some distant explosion:

"I loved Amos Ratcliffe."

Captain Stadger picked up two sheets of oblong paper on the top of his desk, folded them tightly together, and rose. There was no expression on his face, beyond the heaviness of his eyelids.

Daniel Haws tried to look up into the eyes of his officer. Then he sensed that the captain would allow this intimacy, not removing his own eyes at all from the soldier's desperate scrutiny, allowing Daniel so to speak to gaze immodestly and at will into that unknown pair of cold blue eyes so that he might apprehend, rather than have to be told, all that was ready and in store for him as a result of his reply to the captain's interrogation.

"I love Amos Ratcliffe," the soldier now said in a heavy rush of air that escaped from his lungs, and his voice came out now totally changed and as deep as if it had risen from the bottom of a shaft.

He turned his eyes slightly away from his interrogator, and at the same instant he heard the captain's "Dismissed, Private Haws."

Daniel saluted, pivoted, held himself rigid a moment, then marched in perfect cadence out away from the tent.

Once you have admitted a fearful thing to another ear, there may be at first a kind of relief, and then the fearful thing is made more awful by reason of the stranger who knows your secret. Daniel Haws felt intense relief at having given up his secret, even though to such an obvious enemy as Captain Stadger, a man who, he was certain, would with pleasure eat his heart with garlic. But then the first peace that came from no longer carrying his burden alone was suddenly doubled, quadrupled by the anxious dread of an enemy's possessing the secret.

Sitting on a stool erect as a granite pillar in his tent, a day or so later, while Daniel Haws stood at attention before him (the captain almost never gave the words "At ease"), Stadger indicated he wanted Private Haws to go over the "entire story" with him in some detail.

"After all, I'm not going to have you burn . . . I'm going to protect you," Captain Stadger grinned. "You got nothing to fear from me. I like you, Haws, and I think you like me."

Attempting to look into the officer's eyes, Daniel's mind went back to the distant days in the mine when he had looked up into the black shaft and had seen nothing. His pupils likewise now seemed incapable of focussing on the captain.

"What do you say to our agreement?" He heard Stadger's voice, and to his astonishment he perceived for the first time its similarity to the tones of Amos, when that boy had been most grave with him.

"Sir?" Daniel's voice came after the officer called back his wandering attention by a sudden movement of his hand on the desk.

"An agreement," the captain went on, "by which you put yourself entirely into my hands in all and every matter, and surrender your trust to me."

Daniel stared before him.

"You're willing to agree to that, I'm sure, in view of the way things now stand?"

The soldier blinked, did not answer.

"A man who would present himself without his clothes on before his officer's bunk on his first night's arrival in camp," the captain spoke just loud enough to make himself heard.

Incredulous at what he had heard, Daniel looked into the officer's eyes, and could only believe that what Stadger spoke had been the truth, but he cried out nonetheless: "That was not the case, surely, sir!"

"You don't mean to excuse yourself then under the guise of sleepwalking?" Stadger raised his voice ever so slightly and suddenly touched the packet of letters which he had taken from Daniel's barracks bags.

"Sleepwalking, sir?" Daniel's mouth broke into a grin of horror, as the old forgotten charge stirred dimly in his mind. "I never recall sleepwalking in my life, sir."

"Then you never presented yourself stark naked as a

nail that night in my tent, Private Haws?" As the captain spoke, a whole wave of terrible and unknown memories swept over the soldier's flickering consciousness.

Shifting, the captain went on, as his charge hung helpless now on every syllable:

"You say you were the son of coal miners," Captain Stadger mused. "Don't suppose you might have had as much formal schooling therefore as you might have wished, though you tried to better yourself in Chicago . . ."

Daniel Haws remained at attention, but his eyes showed that he was hearing now almost nothing.

"The army is looking for good men, you know, Haws, in this unlimited national emergency. Men like you . . . You been in service before, haven't you now?"

Daniel Haws, frozen speechless, blinked again.

"I said, haven't you!" the captain raised his voice.

Extending one arm, then dropping it against the creases of his trousers, Daniel spoke: "I didn't love Amos Ratcliffe the way you may be thinking, Captain Stadger, sir . . ." His tone was of sudden passionate beseeching. His face had gone an awful yellow, the wrinkles on his brow and around his eyes gathered now like nets.

"What are you talking about, Private Haws?" Captain Stadger inquired, a groundswell of some unknown feeling in his voice. "I'm sure I don't know."

"What I confessed to you, sir."

"You haven't confessed to a thing to me, Private Haws. Whatever you may have told me you told me as a friend. Such as your telling me, say, that you were in the army before, and left by the door of AWOL, and never returned till now, under another name. In one ear, out the other, Haws. Because you were talking to a friend, you see. Not just an army officer. A true friend . . . We'll get to know each other, you and I. You're coming clear to me, Haws. Maybe we might even take a few little trips together, by and by. . . . Not as officer and enlisted man but as two friends with a lot in common . . ."

"I didn't love Amos Ratcliffe with my body, sir! That's what I wanted to say. I never loved him so, sir!"

"How did you love the cocksucker?" Captain Stadger leaped up from his stool like a wire suddenly galvanized into white hot death.

Daniel Haws did not see the look of kindled rage and madness on the face of the captain. If he had, and had he understood, he would have gone over the hill as soon as the captain dismissed him, and he would have done well to do so. All he could see at that moment was the face of Amos Ratcliffe as he had looked when he last took his leave of him in his rooming house in Chicago.

"I loved him as myself," Daniel finished.

Captain Stadger then struck the private with all the accumulated force of a man made criminal by all the hard years behind him and the hate and need.

"You'll love who you're told to love, you fucking bastard, and you'll talk about what we decide to talk about!"

The spectacle of the blood pouring from Daniel's face and mouth calmed the officer. He was affable again. "You may use your handkerchief," Captain Stadger nodded to him.

Haws wiped his mouth and face. The sight of his own blood and in such quantity calmed him also, for tears were not his forte, and he was grateful he could bleed. Captain Stadger handed him another handkerchief he pulled quickly from his own pocket, after Haws had filled the first one.

"I can see we will understand each other, Private Haws." The captain advanced now within an inch of his face. "The army is funny this way. If a man cooperates, his life can be relatively easy, relatively smooth. Things run on and come to an end. But if the man resists and can't take command," and Daniel felt with the thrill of unbelief iron fingers closing over his broken mouth and lips, as Stadger held him in savage embrace, "if he resists there's hardly a thing that don't happen to him until he's broke down to the bone."

Removing his fingers from the soldier's mouth, he waited for Haws's "Yes, sir."

"While you, Daniel," Eustace Chisholm wrote to the APO in Biloxi, Mississippi, "are being devilled by Captain Stadger, or at least you make out you are at death's crumbling door, your Amos, about whom you beg so frequently for news, is, I am happy to report, flourishing like a whole peninsula of green bay trees.

"I am only," Ace's letter continued, "if the truth must be told, half sorry for you because though your persecutor may have uncovered your weak spot, he has been summoned to be your judge by you yourself, Daniel Haws. Like all the martyrs in history, you have presented yourself at his bench before your case was ever called, and without so much as a touch from his white-hot iron on your so-receptive flesh, you have confessed your crime: 'Yes, captain, I am the lover of Amos. Yes, sir, that photograph is of the boy who stole my heart away.' If you had told him the full truth, how you left your love, after killing it in the bud, and chickened out of Chicago, maybe even a Captain Stadger would not have the yen to put the poker to your palpitating asshole . . .

"Yes, you who was so wise, so prudent, so clever, such a

miser, so careful for your reputation and future, now look at you. Well, when Troy falls, it falls to charred ruins, with nothing left for anybody to poke around in.

"But I started out in this letter to tell you how Amos is flourishing. He not only never looked better—his flesh gives the appearance of having been bathed in fresh strawberry juice, his teeth sparkle, eyes shine, but the thing that has perhaps astonished everybody, stranger, friend, foe, is his ability to wear a wardrobe. Believe you me, the heir of Sampford Court, during the period of his being smitten on your little dagger-mate, bought him a sizable one: shirts of sea-island cotton, custom-made of course, ties from India, shoes hand-made in rugged Scotland. Even his arm pits give off some perfume that costs easily eighty dollars for ten drops; he has now stepped out of the Arabian Nights entertainment, but he is entertaining nobody but himself. He can't begin to count his lovers, now he is free of old Reuben. Yet I must tell you he is not spoiled or conceited. In fact I can see something is weighing him down, but whatever it is now he would be in the same situation in any case where you left him: the only thing he ever wanted and still wants is you, and so he has even less than when his toes and ass were out and he smelled like a goat . . ."

Carefully tearing up Ace's letter, Daniel allowed the paper to fall into the blue-green waters of the Mississippi Sound.

"You shouldn't throw away an interesting document like that," he heard the deep, slightly quavering voice behind him.

He did not need to turn around to know who it was.

"Yes, sir."

Daniel rose from the grass.

"I want you to save me all your letters from this time on." Captain Stadger stepped forward to face him. "That way we can be sure they won't fall into the hands of an outside party who might not understand . . ."

21

Carla Chisholm's Golgotha was made complete, if not entirely unendurable, the August following her return to Chicago by a change in Eustace that made all her other troubles seem minor and her money worries minuscule. Her job still brought home enough to keep her and Ace in grub, with a roof over their heads, an occasional movie, and more frequently (since Ace walked so much) shoe repairs, though there always came that period of a week or so just before pay day when, despite her scraping and tithing, there wasn't a red cent in the house (Eustace was more extravagant than ever, stealing away to a good many boxing matches, and handing out nickels and dimes to bums), and they had to go to bed without supper. A diet of tea and crackers gives one, the first day or so, the vague feeling of having eaten. Later, one wakes up in the middle of the night with a sour stomach and hunger pangs. Carla, sleepless from burdens, would go out into the kitchen at 2:00 A.M. to think things over, leaving her husband also sleepless in bed, perhaps more uncomfortable than she was, for he was more active physically and his poorly shod feet had covered miles along the Lake Front, over museum floors, and down alleys, clutching always his poem to hell, matted together now with sheets of PX letter paper, which smelled of Army, in the fine delicate handwriting of Private Daniel Haws.

What minimized all the other accidents of Carla Chisholm's chagrins and sorrows was, to put it simply, her growing certainty that her husband was going insane. He had always been a more or less professional madman according to the dictates of his calling—she understood that, of course. She based her definition of actual insanity on the following series of events.

It began after he told her that the Negro psychic, Luwana Edwards, had passed on her "Mantle" of second sight to him when Luwana had given up telling fortunes for a living and entered standard religious work. Carla had smiled then at what he said, perhaps giggled.

Then only a few days after he had told her about the "Mantle," he began seeing events before they transpired, in earnest. As in a home movie, the things transpiring in Biloxi, Mississippi (which Luwana had already seen months before and as a result had refused to tell Daniel Haws's fortune) all unreeled before Ace's half-startled half-bored eyes. For example, he "got" the name, Captain Stadger; he saw his round face, framed with an aureole of blond hair; he even described his hands, strong to the point of being nearly misshapen. All this before one word of Stadger came in the PX letters.

As if, then, to prove to Carla that his "gift" was real and not a literary attitude, he would quote from Daniel's letters before they ever reached Chicago. He also reported conversations being held near Cobden, Illinois by Cousin Ida; he said that Maureen O'Dell was to marry Reuben Masterson before that item appeared in the society columns, and he foresaw the terrible thing to befall Amos.

But chiefly his second sight was limited to Biloxi, and from his dirt-stained apartment windows he watched both the principal drama and took in the tropical backdrop—saw the pelicans on the Misssissippi Sound, smelled azaleas and magnolias, touched the palms and the live oaks with the moss. He remembered without knowing that there had once lived down there Indians who passed the time of day in the shade of those oaks on the shore of the Bay. He looked in on the factory that was solely devoted to the manufacture of paper flowers for the Day of the Dead, and passed by the old Biloxi Cemetery with its strange construction of canopies over the graves.

Often in the middle of the night, pressed against his wife, Eustace would wake with a start, and throw off his quilt, spellbound by the encounter between Captain Stadger and Daniel Haws. With helpless sick terror he saw the moon face of the officer bent over the soldier, while from a mouth which looked too well-shaped to form such words he heard: "Private Haws, burglars use diamond-tipped drills to get at their treasure. Know what I'll use to get mine from you?"

Carla, so trained in the rationalism and liberalism of the epoch and partisan to its simple-minded definition of human nature, finally could only turn away from her husband. She had been able to stand all his other failings, but his having even an unwilling relationship with the "unknown" began to estrange her at last from him, jeopardize her love itself. She thus took refuge in the explanation he was insane.

Eustace should have been glad therefore that Amos returned to him at such a time. Yet occupied as he was with Daniel, he was less grateful than he might have been otherwise. He turned to Amos now principally because Carla refused to pursue his experiences any further. Had he been less interested in Daniel at that moment, he might also have warned Rat of the fateful thing that was about to overtake him, but he missed it until almost the moment of the event itself.

When the two had resumed "running" together again, an incident took place which amused and delighted both Ace and Amos. Incessant walkers as ever, they were meandering along the Lake Front one afternoon, when a natty policeman stopped them and asked Amos (still in his Masterson wardrobe) if the older poorly dressed gent had propositioned him. Taken aback, Amos had tried to explain that Ace and he were old friends. The cop, however, incredulous, had separated them, and after giving Amos a lecture on the perils of picking up rough trade told him to go home.

Catching up with one another a few minutes after the brush with the police, the two walked on together in moody silence.

Eustace insisted suddenly on stopping in front of a Bethel Mission, near Sixty-third street, to inspect the wording of a sign:

DEAR GOD, THROW YOUR STRONG ARMS OF PROTECTION AROUND THE TRUE WIDOWS AND AGED PEOPLES OF THE WORLD, AND DO NOT AVERT YOUR EYES FROM OUR ARMY OF YOUNG MEN, MANY HARDLY MORE THAN BOYS.

"I've got something bad to tell you," Eustace mumbled. Amos waited, worry lines about his eyes and over the bridge of his nose.

"I've turned into a Goddamned Negro spiritualist," Eustace said.

After a long walk they had reached the rocks which were piled fifteen or twenty feet high above the water of the lake.

They sat down, remembering how less desperate and much happier, after all, they had used to feel when they sat here the year before, and yet how desperate they had been then too. A few gulls hovered near some refuse floating on the oil-stained water.

"I hear and see everything Daniel tells me even before his letters get here with the news," Eustace began.

Amos nodded.

"I can't help it, it's so." Ace defended himself for the first time in Amos's memory. "Carla kept count of the coincidences for a time, my knowing an event in Mississippi before Daniel confirmed it in a later letter, but she's given up keeping count now. Wouldn't be surprised she ran out on me again . . . I see this Captain Stadger, for example, he's the one who's going to do something to Daniel Haws, probably kill him. Then the damned letter comes, with the PX smell, the desperate handwriting but intelligent message. Why didn't Daniel stay in the coal mines? We'd both be a hell of a lifetime better off . . ."

Amos bowed his head, squinted his eyes, and looked toward South Chicago, from which one could see clearly even at this daylight hour the steel works belching out foundations of sparks from the Bessemer converters.

"Captain Stadger is bushwhacking Daniel Haws," Eustace said.

Amos winced, bowed his head.

"I forgot you still feel strong so about him," Ace mumbled, throwing a stone hard into the lake. "What I'm telling you then, Amos, is that the old nigger woman, when she renounced her second sight for the sake of her Church, by Christ, put her powers on me. Handed me her Mantle. I'm bedevilled and bewitched, and I'm getting everything that happens to Daniel Haws as soon as it happens to him. Cap-

tain Stadger is going to tear his guts out, and I'm the mes-
senger of the event sent by the Lord . . ."

Amos sat immobile, growing paler. Eustace punched him
sharply.

"We're being observed again," Ace pointed out.
"Damned police squad car has been tailing us over here
. . . Cops can't understand why anybody is ever out of his
workshop, house or penitentiary . . . Besides, I'm in rags
compared to your ill-gotten finery . . ."

"I can't quit remembering how nice we used to think it
was here in the summer, on these rocks," Amos said.

"Yes, sweetheart," Ace replied, "but that was when we
both had someone to love us."

"Ace, do you have the syph?" Amos asked swiftly, looking back briefly at the squad car which just then decided,
after all, to leave.

"There go the yellow bastards," Ace said. "They run out
of niggers to pick on, and only your good clothes kept them
off us. They still think I picked you up, Rat. How do you
like that?"

Eustace lay back on the rocks now and squinting looked
at the saffron tinged cumulus clouds skirting by. "I had the
syphilis, yes, sweet Amos, but that isn't why I've got second
sight, so don't try to explain it like some shitty intellectual."

"Did they cure you?" Amos kept at it.

"Oh, I suppose they must have," Ace said. "See how spry
I am?" He grasped his penis firmly in his hand and showed
its outlines beneath his thin trousers.

"You're not pulling the wool over my eyes then, Ace,
about you seeing all them things in Mississippi . . ."

"Wish I was." Ace sprang up from his lolling position on
the rocks. "Wish oh wish I was! It's the strict bone-bred
truth, Rat. When that old nigger put off her Mantle, it fell

right on my shapely shoulders. And here's where you come in, Amos darling . . . I got to get rid of the Mantle and you're the one to help me."

Stopping before he went on with a description of his "plan," Eustace stared an unaccustomed length of time at the boy, then added:

"Amos Ratcliffe, do you know something? You are beautiful. You have posed a long time as a scholar and, Christ, you are bright, but let me tell you something, you can make it better as a whore. Masterson wasn't up to your level, that's why that went wrong. Though we all laugh about his coming wedding with old Maureen, that's more his speed then you. But you can find yourself somebody who will really pay for you. I mean your face only comes a couple of times in a century, why you're a fucking Antinoüs. Get all the money you can while you still look like a sunflower of the gods, and give me just enough to get this black woman's gift off me. That's all I ask . . . But regardless of me, and my little problem, you've got a gift but it's a gift that don't last. I never said this to you before, or to anybody, but you do look like God Almighty. Sell your ass, Amos, while you can."

Ace got up and brushed his clothes.

"See that funny bird over there with that awful pair of eyes. That's a bustard." They both laughed. "That's right," Ace said, "a bustard."

"Stand up and let me look at you again," Eustace said after a moment. "Good. Now let me tell you how you can help me. We'll go back to my den as my noble wife is out working . . ."

Back in Ace's apartment, Amos looked at his friend and all of a sudden could see the truth of what the poet was talking about. He saw the change that had taken place in

Ace since Daniel had run off and he himself had gone to live those few weeks with Reuben. Old Eus was really going down hill.

Without offering Amos so much as a glass of water in way of refreshment, Eustace went right to the core of his trouble.

"I have not been a nigger-haunter since my earliest youth, way back when you were at your mother's breast." Amos heard Ace's voice from his seated position on the floor, and could not suppress a yawn. "Again, Amos, old child, I felt the need of rinsing out my brain of those letters I was getting from your renegade lover, those confessions, those tales from Magnolia, Mississippi, and before I knew it—this was not very long ago—I had walked as if in my sleep to South Parkway. There I was alone with 233,903 Negroes, having emerged unscathed from the 371 acres of the largest inland black park in the city, with the Poro College Negro School of Beauty sign staring me in the face.

"I went right up the stone steps to Luwana's front parlor and rang. No answer, of course. I looked in through the window at the furniture draped as per usual with the white sheets, with incense burning before a statue of a saint (she combines all religions under one roof). I knew Luwana Edwards alias Stella Martin alias Ruby Watkins alias Emma Green was in that house alive . . . I rang and rang, and finally, as if she had been behind it all that time, she opened the door. Scared, I guess.

"She let me come in. 'You've felt the change in yourself, then,' she came right to the point, without turning around to face me.

" 'I'm getting these terrible letters from Mississippi,' I said, 'and I happen to know you are from Biloxi yourself originally, Miss Watkins.'

" 'I'm sorry you ain't appreciative of a gift like that which I done give you not without a lot of thought and which many a man would give his all to have.'

" 'Name one,' " I said.

" 'Well,' she said, looking down at her house-slippers, 'Mister Chisholm, it was destiny. I thought a writer, just the same, would get a lot out of my gift.'

"That stumped me," Eustace said, rising, walking the floor now in earnest in front of Amos. He was picking his teeth with an old goose-quill toothpick, probably because he had run out of snuff.

" 'I done give you the gift of my Mantle, second sight,' she said, as if I needed to have it explained again. 'But, Mr. Chisholm, I don't know no way of you givin' it back to me, if that's why you keep comin' here to see me. Ain't no way I ever heard of.'

" 'I'm not leaving your house until you think of a way,' I told her, and I must have looked really portentous, because she began studying hard and even cried a little, the silent kind of bawling I don't mind, I guess it was sincere, and then she came up with her little proposal.

" 'For a hundred dollars, Mister Chisholm, I think I can work out something for you.'

" 'Sounds like maybe blackmail, don't it?' I said, but there was no real conviction in my voice, I was too desperate to turn anything down and she knew it.

" 'Blackmail, rabbits,' she scoffed. 'You know me better than that, Mister Chisholm. We has to pray the Mantle away from you and that take a congregation in session prayin' for twenty-four hours solid. Most of them is workin' people, can't just sit and pray without no recompense, and you know it . . . One hundred dollars is a bottom minimum, Mister Chisholm.'

"I got up, then," Eustace finished, "and thought of everybody I could think of to give me the hundred. I even called your old lover Masterson. He's all busy with wedding plans, and by the time he hung up I was beginning to feel like lending him money, he talked so poor . . .

"Amos," Eustace took the boy's hands and kissed each palm, "go out and get old Eus a hundred crisp new bills and get me off this hot seat. In the name of the love you bear Daniel Haws, please?"

Amos got up and looked at Ace, and the look said he would do it.

That was the last time Eustace ever set eyes on Amos Ratcliffe alive.

22

From a work detail in the midst of the thickest part of foliage, Daniel Haws wiped the sweat from his eyelids to be sure that he was actually seeing in a clearing twenty yards away Captain Stadger, immobile, unaffected by the atrocious heat, standing with his unmoving hands emerging from starched cuffs, holding a letter, reading attentively.

Putting down his shovel, without asking permission from the detail sergeant, Daniel, dressed only in fatigue trousers, found himself in the presence of Stadger, hardly aware he had left without authorization.

Near where the captain stood reading, another detail of men were pounding iron posts into the ground with sledgehammers. On a kind of short green picnic table, occasionally used down here for officers' mess, Daniel's straining eyes caught sight of a sheaf of envelopes, which he identified in panic as having been addressed to him. The letter now fluttering in the Gulf breeze in the captain's hand, almost certainly, he knew, contained a message written solely for him.

"Information is coming through nicely, Haws," the captain spoke, ignoring Daniel's standing there unasked and without permission.

A drone of insects in the clump of bushes sounded heavily, echoed by the feeble cry of birds from more distant green thickets.

The captain suddenly looked up from his reading, his eyes fixed on Daniel's uncovered chest.

"Developed yourself quite a bit in the coal mines, didn't you?" The captain kept his eyes on his body. "Or is it just the Cherokee Indian in your blood after all?

"Whatever the hell it is, best go back and tell your sergeant I've specially requested you." The captain looked off now towards nowhere in particular.

Daniel did as he was ordered and the work sergeant felt piqued that Captain Stadger had taken a man from his detail without proper procedure, and looked angrily toward the officer, swearing under his breath.

When he returned, Daniel found the captain's eyes fixed on the other more distant detail of men pounding iron bars into the earth with sledgehammers. Suddenly whistles sounded from different parts of the camp, giving notice of the end of the work period, and details of men all around fell out and returned in procession to their own squads.

"Have ourselves a nice quiet private stretch of land to read our letters in, Haws . . . Sit down, why don't you?" the captain invited him.

There was now such an unearthly stillness about them

that Daniel almost felt there was no army camp at all and that there had never been any soldiers working nearby on detail minutes before.

"Here's a pad and a sharp pencil for you," the captain laid these on the picnic table by Daniel. The soldier stirred uneasily.

"By the way," the officer began, "this little letter I have been reading so carefully here in the great outdoors is signed Amos Ratcliffe."

The captain then looked up, and his eyes fixed on Haws.

"Best put something over them prize muscles of yours, though, before you come down with some new fever or other, and we have to ship you back suddenly to the hospital," the captain said.

Daniel jerked his fatigue jacket over his shoulders.

"Give me your undivided attention now, Haws."

"Please don't read me the letter, sir," Daniels' voice came, choking.

Taking no notice of the outburst, the captain read slowly, deliberately, almost syllable by syllable while Daniel stared incredulous, wild-eyed at the innocent-looking thin letter paper as deadly to him now as escaping poison gas.

He hardly heard the first part of the letter with its childish description of their "old times" together in the rooming-house, Amos's disappointments with the Mastersons, his worries and indecisions, his "heartbreak." Only the last sentences, read to him with agonizing halting tempo, as if beaten upon his eardrums by the soldiers bearing the sledgehammers, were audible to him:

No matter what happens in the future days, or weeks, Daniel—and I am going now to try to find some kind of job, probably back home—remember out of all my life it was only you I looked up to and cared for. All I can say, and I got to say it, is you were the only one I ever have loved. Don't forget that, even if you forget me.

Yours ever, Amos.

Daniel's head had slipped over so that it rested now on the picnic table, lifeless and unmoving as if it had been severed.

Captain Stadger's fingers lifted his head up, and pushed it back methodically, and the officer's voice, when he spoke, had a chilling almost gentle calm:

"I want for you to answer this letter, right here and now, Haws, so I can put it in the mail. Hear? That's what the paper and sharpened pencil are for."

"Don't make me do that, sir." The soldier shot a glance of imploring helplessness that would have softened perhaps any other man, and Haws's hand grasping a lead pencil broke it in two pieces. The captain pushed another pencil toward him but the soldier, suddenly seizing the captain's hand, cried with a voice unrecognizable as his own:

"Do anything you want to with me, or make me confess to anything you want, use me any way you now wish, sir, but don't make me write him anything . . ."

"Write that sentence down you just said," the captain cried.

Haws seized the remaining pencil and, in a passionate flourish of letters, obeyed.

Happily, deliriously he handed the paper to the captain who read it eagerly and put it in his stiff jacket.

"Just so you don't ever make me write him," Haws muttered.

"I'll tell you something, Haws." The captain came very close to him now, leaning over the picnic table, one hand

resting on his bent knee. "I'll tell you the truth, too, because you just give me the idea. (You give me more ideas
anyhow than any enlisted man I ever saw.) I'm goin' to
take you over, as you say, and do what you just give me
permission to do."

The captain returned to Amos's letter again, as if the impossible, the incredible had here been expressed in concrete
form for him. It was as if he had not that first time believed
he was hearing aright when, without prompting or torture,
Daniel had confessed to his love for Amos.

"One thing before we part, Private Haws, and please lift
up your chin and look me straight in the eyes."

Daniel obeyed, and the captain drew still closer.

"What would you call this letter I just read to you, from
Amos Ratcliffe?"

Haws swallowed, somehow found the answer: "The letter of a friend."

"You mean you'd call it a perfectly commonplace communication between two men?"

Haws hesitated, somehow got out, "It's what I first said,
sir, the letter from one friend to . . . another."

"You wouldn't say then you are receiving letters from a
degenerate and a blackmailer, and that is why you refuse to
answer him?"

Under Haws's silence, the captain, his anger roused,
raised his voice ever so slightly: "What kind of a person
would you say then wrote you that letter?"

Daniel started to rise, the captain pushed him down, and
the soldier's eyes tried to find something to rest on. In the
dying light, the last flash of day reflected itself on the distant iron stakes that had been pounded into the earth that
afternoon.

Captain Stadger had to repeat his question.

"A troubled person," Daniel replied at last. As he uttered these words, a strange soft peaceful look came over Daniel Haws's face. The remarkable look, so sudden and so unexpected, made the captain pause for a moment.

"Then why couldn't you write as one troubled person to another?" Here the captain's hate and loathing struggled under limited control. "What you told me that day—that you reciprocate his feelings for you . . ."

"I'm not man enough to accept his love," Haws said, but it seemed clear somehow he had not spoken in this case really for the captain.

Then suddenly taking up another packet of letters, this time from Eustace Chisholm, the captain read page after page of damaging testimony against Amos Ratcliffe. Daniel hardly heard it. There was nothing, however, left out in Eustace's letters. They were the letters of a literary man who tries hard to say everything damaging he can about another human being. In the end, one felt he was listening to the speech of the prosecution before the judge and jury.

"Anything to say to all of that?" Captain Stadger asked quietly, folding the papers back into the envelope.

"You don't have no right to read my mail, and you know it," Daniel said, and without permission he rose vehemently. He struck the captain full in the face.

Not so much inflamed perhaps as relieved and grateful, the officer sprang at the younger man's throat and his fingers tore at the flesh, bringing blood.

"I'll break you," the captain said. "I'll put you where you won't see the light of day for the rest of your natural life unless you listen to me . . ."

Recovered from his "daring," Daniel cocked his head like a deaf man who feels the earth explode from under him.

"Do you know what I've got on you?" the captain cried.

Then gaining some control over himself to steady his own maniacal passion, he added: "You gave me permission to do as I saw fit with you if you didn't write the letter I ordered you to Amos Ratcliffe."

Daniel nodded.

"I want you to tell me here and now then that he was a cheap little cocksucker and you never loved him."

Daniel stared implacably at Stadger, while the captain waited. When he saw Daniel's refusal was as stubborn as his earlier one to write the letter, the captain's fists flew in an unrestrained volley over the private's face, desperately unprotected.

"Now let me see you take off that goddamn fatigue suit and any other rags you have under it, and I'm going over you in earnest."

Smiling, almost happily obedient, Daniel began unbuttoning his fatigues, as if at last he was to meet the punishment he would be able to take.

Hardly recognizing himself the next morning after reveille as he looked in the cracked latrine mirror, Daniel Haws at first could scarcely connect his disfigured appearance with the happening in the green clearing outside the area of the pitched tents. It now appeared improbable—for one thing, the outrage had been committed near enough to the camp easily to be observed, even though the light had failed at that particular hour. Daniel's body was a crazy quilt of cuts, slashes and bruises, and everything from his waist down pained sickeningly where Stadger had poured out what seemed to be unappeasable ferocity of longing for this individual soldier's flesh.

The enlisted men who shared their tent with Haws had decided, when they had seen him return after Stadger's assault on him, that the soldier had again been beaten up by outsiders on one of his regular visits to the out-of-bounds Negro sections of town. They left him strictly alone, in grudging silence, perhaps admiration, and considered him probably too tough even for the regular army.

Just before his dismissal from his punishment, Haws remembered now dimly, the captain had given him this speech. Shattered by his own physical exertions over the soldier, the officer had spoken with as much coolness as possible. "I've worked myself to my limits against you tonight, Haws, but you're still granite against me. You give only resistance, while yielding. Against your granite then I've got to find a substitute. I've got to make your hardness yield to some other hardness which I'll have to bring from the outside. Now we've gone this far, neither of us can stop until you give me complete submission . . ."

It should not have been a surprise to Daniel then that on Friday evening a few days later, going out the main entrance of the army post, having recovered sufficiently from his night of beating and planning to hitchhike to New Orleans, Daniel was presenting his two-day pass to an M.P., when a corporal came up and asked for the private's name and serial number.

"Haws is the man who's to be on special detail for the weekend," the corporal said as he checked a list.

"Sorry, soldier." The corporal studied Daniel now with grave attention. "You've been requested for special duty on the post, and can't go on leave."

Returning to his tent, Daniel put down his overnight bag, loosened his tie a bit, then suddenly tied it again with firm strictness. He looked about the camp, already more than half-deserted.

He walked slowly back to the place of the recent "encounter," saw the picnic table on which the letters had been placed, and where he had written out his abdication to the authority of the captain, and a choking sensation gripped his throat.

At the same time Daniel understood that he was now hunting *him*, and this realization froze him with horror.

As he walked towards the waters of the Sound, he wondered whether he should not just go out swimming and never come back.

Stumbling about in the underbrush, he came to another little clearing which he would have sworn had not been there before. It was close enough to the water so that some of the Sound's shimmering surface emerged through the leafage, and here a long mess table had been recently placed, freshly painted. At the end of the table, his hands resting on the new green coating, immobile as a waxworks dummy, sat Captain Stadger, a billy club near his left starched-sleeved hand.

"What does this place remind you of?" the captain inquired, his voice only loud enough to carry to the soldier, still some yards away.

Daniel walked on up to the seated captain.

"I remember picnics, I guess, sir, at county fairgrounds," the soldier replied. He saluted then at a warning glance from his officer.

"I'm glad you got such a good memory, Haws," the captain said gently after a pause. Although some flies had lit and sat motionless on the face of the officer as he spoke, he made no effort to chase them away, and Daniel found himself gazing at Stadger's hands. For such powerful instruments superbly fitted to torture, they now looked only beautifully shaped, symmetrical, almost white and harmless. Except for a deep scratch on the right one, the result of their struggle together, they were unmarked, but even this was the result, chiefly accidental, of Haws's frantic determination to give the captain every ceded right to torture him to the limit short of making him write Amos of his love. Actually the scratch had been self-inflicted when the captain had mistaken Haws's movements of compliance for those of aggression.

"The army needs men with good memories," he heard the captain speak again. The officer rose now, smiling faintly.

"Picnics in the county fairgrounds," he repeated Daniel's remark.

Turning now to face the soldier, the officer spoke suddenly with fierce inflection: "You and me will have picnics galore together."

Daniel bent his head forward in a nod. There was a kind of yellow tone under his tanned skin today, and his thick straight hair seemed suddenly covered with Amos's macassar oil, but it was sweat pouring out of his scalp.

"The colonel gave you to me on special detail for the whole weekend," Stadger mumbled, as if careless whether his words were audible to Haws. "So let's just mosey about in the brush here, wait for the light to fail a bit, and see where we might pick us a picnic site for now or future outings."

Suddenly wheeling about abruptly, as if some alarm had rung, the captain said, "You go ahead, first now, Haws."

A flood of childhood memories swarmed over Daniel as he and the officer now walked into the thickest part of the foliage. He remembered in detail one deserted county fairground in particular after the picnicking season was at an end and the concessions and the grounds themselves had been closed.

In the hot still August afternoon, he could hear an oven-bird with its little cry of "Teacher! teacher!" and in the distance the note of a waterthrush.

"A *beautiful place when twilight casts its spell on the tropical waters*," Captain Stadger quoted a tourist guide-book on the Gulf, in a voice of terrible expressionless calm.

When they had got into another section of vegetation, where the stillness was even more deadly, Stadger told Daniel to halt.

"Did you notice whether or not I was wearing sidearms?" The captain spoke to the soldier's back.

Daniel did not reply, and he dared not turn around.

"Don't tell me you're as pisspoor an observer as you are a soldier. Turn around and look."

Daniel obeyed, and the captain touched his revolver in its holster.

"I only hope I won't have to use this on you tonight," the captain said. "Come over here, Haws . . . Now take hold of this revolver and then pull it out from the holster."

Daniel did so.

"Now put the revolver back in its holster."

Again Daniel obeyed.

"You done that pretty well," the captain complimented him. "Your mouth trembled, but your fucking hands were still."

"Now face ahead again," the captain commanded. "Walk ten paces and stop."

Daniel did so.

A small black non-poisonous snake darted across his path while he executed the paces, and a kind of rejoicing relief came over him to see a living creature at this moment.

"By the by, do you know what is done to a soldier who

has syphilis and don't report it, Private Haws?" The captain's voice came from a seeming great distance, further, Daniel felt, than the ten paces.

"They courtmartial him, sir."

"Do you have syphilis, Private Haws?"

The soldier paused, looked into the giant oaks, saw some of the blue sparkle of the Mississippi Sound.

"You wouldn't want to be courtmartialed would you, Haws, for refusing to give needed information?"

"No," Haws muttered.

"No, or no sir?"

Daniel refused to answer.

"The army is interested in a lot of things about you," the captain ignored his disobedience. "I could tell the army more about you, but it knows enough for the time being."

A long period of silence passed then in which Daniel again had the sensation, as in his previous encounter with Stadger, of having gone deaf. He did not seem to hear even the birds now or the oaks moving in the breeze, and no movement, not even of breath, from the captain.

Then he heard the command.

"Drop your pants and shorts and don't fall forward until I knock you forward."

Daniel obeyed.

"I didn't want you to think this hospital report which just come in to me today that says there is a possibility of you having a dose together with malaria scares me from exercising my authority over you, especially in view of the fact I have permission from you to do all I do, in writing." Stadger spoke almost in one breath.

When Haws did not reply, he pistol-whipped him smartly.

As if in response to this new punishment, Daniel now methodically removed all his clothing, including his shoes and socks, still facing forward.

As if maddened anew at the sight of his rich brown flesh, the captain now whipped him with the pistol across the shoulder blades and spine and buttocks.

After the first savage embraces with his own flesh and the satisfied hardly human outcry of relief from the captain, there was a pause. Then a strange sound came, as if from a whirring of metallic wings. At first Daniel thought he was being attacked with the billy club which in the captain's powerful hands was being used for this new excruciating torment, but looking back against his orders, before he felt the correcting pistol whip his face, he saw an iron instrument of unbelievable medieval shape and monstrous design, held in the captain's other hand and thrusting itself now into Daniel's body, the first of the "real" instruments, he supposed, to be used in breaking him down to "submission."

For minutes of unendurable hell the soldier, impaled as it were by the iron piece and prevented from falling forward, tasted the most exquisite torment he could have ever imagined his body capable of in his wildest imaginings.

The thick felt body of a moth on his lips awakened Daniel, and opening an eye—half of his face was pressed tight to the ground—he saw the "fair-browed Moon" about which Amos had once written in a poem addressed to him. Another line of the poem came to him, where Amos had called the moon the eternal sleepwalker.

Sitting up, in hideous pain, he noticed the presence of many other heavy-bodied moths. It was not really dark any more, and the water of the Sound, seen through the trees, had already caught a pink light.

He rose to go back to his tent and grimly remembered that the pain he felt now was hardly, after all, greater than on those bitter mornings when as a boy he had to descend into the coal mine, shuttling down into the dark as to destruction.

A kind of grim satisfaction came over him that he had been so frightfully, so hideously injured by Stadger for no purpose or meaning. It confirmed somehow everything he felt about man and life.

He stopped at the edge of the clearing and saw the row of tents. Leaning over, he wiped some blood off his army boot and cleaned his hand on the grass.

He suddenly felt exultant. He wanted Captain Stadger to finish the job now he had begun. He didn't want to live. He had never wanted to live. The thought had always come bobbing up into his mind like an imaginary cork that reaches the surface once in a blue moon; now the cork floated visible, palpable, almost entirely out of water, in plain view. He had never wanted to be alive.

He then heard his mouth pronounce the one word, "Amos".

That had been the only time he had ever been alive.

He knew he was going to be all right where the captain was concerned. He would be able to stand anything now from his hands, he would not fail to give the officer the total satisfaction he required and expected of him, for Daniel had what both Amos and the captain must have been powerless not to linger over, a perfection—compact of blood, bone, flesh—that was the target attracting destruction.

He got back to his tent in time to stand reveille.

After the roll-call, his sergeant came over to him, looked at him quizzically, and said, "Your Captain Stadger wants to see you in the headquarters room."

At that time, in a stealthy manner that betokened perhaps some faint understanding of the soldier's predicament, the sergeant handed him two letters, just arrived, addressed to him. One, Daniel saw, without surprise or even interest now, was from Ace; the other was a black-bordered letter from Ida Henstridge.

Walking toward the headquarters squad room, he veered, went over to the mess hall, saw with satisfaction they had side bacon and fried potatoes and grits, took generous helpings and sat down with the strong black chicory coffee, munched, shook his head, opened Ace's letter.

He had hardly read the salutation when a corporal came over to him and told him Captain Stadger wanted to see him. "Tell him I'm reading my morning mail," Daniel answered.

A string of obscene expostulations came from the corporal, who knew better than to take such a message to the captain and remained at Daniel's side.

The letter from Ace, to which Daniel now turned his attention, at first seemed to make no sense, so startling was its news, and as he finished it he realized he had not really comprehended its contents. Trying to reread it he seemed to see only blank spaces. Badly confused now, he turned to Amos's mother's letter as if to find explanation there. Written from a funeral parlor, Ida Henstridge's letter spoke of Amos's sad "passing," the expenses of his "service," which she had had to pay for out of her savings, and went on to a description of the funeral ceremony conducted by Reverend McIlhenny.

Daniel then returned to Ace's letter, and read:

I will have myself to blame, I suppose for the rest of my life, along with my other misdeeds, for having sent Amos to pay off that old black nigger fortune-teller so she would remove the Mantle of Second Sight from me. I never dreamed he would go there, and succeed, and of course never dreamed he would be shot as he came out by a policeman mistaking him for a housebreaker.

Aren't you getting my letters, Daniel?

Please believe me, I never meant he should go over to the district or pay her off. I was only joking.

Why aren't you answering my letters? Maybe they are keeping them from you. Should I go on writing?

Just to think, our Amos has already been in the ground now for over a week, and we'll never set eyes on that fellow again . . .

"Do you want to report to sick call?" Daniel heard the corporal's voice over him. He had slipped down from where he was seated to the floor, hardly without realizing it. He had not fainted, for his eyes were open.

Moving slightly, Daniel shook his head, took the corporal's extended hand, and stood up stiffly as if at attention before an officer.

"Fever maybe," the corporal said.

Daniel shook his head, persuaded the corporal he could leave him, and when the non-com had left he stumbled over to the PX, where he inquired of the soldier-clerk if they sold thermometers.

"Only to officers," the clerk informed him.

"This is for Captain Stadger," Daniel told the bare-faced lie.

The clerk nodded, eyes oblique, and handed Haws a thermometer without wrapping it up.

Going into the latrine, Haws hesitated a moment,

whether he should determine his temperature here or go into the woods where there was less likely to be anybody to watch, then inserted the glass tube carefully in his mouth, and stepped over to a stall to urinate.

Pissing slowly, he heard the voice, "Watch it, soldier."

He stopped wetting for a minute.

"Get your cock away from that wall, it's covered with lime, and if another of you bastards goes on sick call for lye on your prick, you'll be courtmartialed."

Daniel Haws nodded to the non-com shouting at him, began to urinate slowly again clear of the wall, finished, dried his hands on his khaki handkerchief, then took the thermometer slowly out of his mouth and shook it carefully. He blinked, shook it again, gazed slowly. It read 104° F. The thermometer must be busted, he figured.

Outside he found his way to a shady clump of bushes, lay back, smoothed out Eustace's letter, read and read again the message.

"Rat," he called, as he lay back holding the thin pages.

He saw the army boots out of the corner of his eyes. He closed his eyes tight, then heard the captain's voice.

Rising to salute him, Daniel felt, as in a revelation, that he was seeing the officer for the first time. What now attracted his eye was not the captain's hands, but his smooth fair face, the blond straight hair as yellow as cornsilk; whereas before he had seen him as without age, Daniel saw him now almost as youthful as Amos, and at that moment of looking at him, Stadger showed no trace of cruelty on a face smooth as a linen sheet.

"If you've been fixing to go on sick call, you can forget it." The captain's voice was so disparate from the impression his face had just given. "I can cure you of anything amiss with you. Besides the colonel has assigned you to me indefinitely . . . No more KP for you, Haws." He laughed.

Daniel pushed the thermometer toward him.

The captain grasped it without reading it, placed it in his jacket. He yawned lazily at Daniel.

"Dismissed," The captain's voice seemed to come from a great distance.

By some tremendous exertion, Daniel was able to bring his hand to his forehead in some vague similitude of a salute, heard his own heels click, then smiling faintly felt himself sprawling at the officer's effulgent shoes.

Wakening, he found himself in some heavily wooded section of the camp, rife with the whirl of insects. Looking about, he saw Stadger lying beside him in his immaculate starched trousers and jacket, but with a touch of grass stain on one leg. Shading his eyes, trying to get his bearings, Daniel realized with certainty that the officer would have had to carry him here. In the pocket of the captain's jacket he recognized the letters from Eustace and Ida Henstridge.

"What'll you do when the bullets start whizzing, if you pass out like this in training camp, Haws?" the captain's voice inquired.

Lunging suddenly, Daniel tried to grasp the stolen letters resting in the captain's pocket, but Stadger caught the soldier's hand in mid-air and flung it back.

Removing his revolver from his belt, he held it indifferently now in his left hand, while with his other hand he pushed Haws back against the grass, and leaned over him for what seemed an eternity, lost in concentration like one reading a difficult map. Daniel kept his eyes tightly closed, waiting whatever the captain might now elect to bestow on him.

"Open your eyes and look at me, Mr. Walk-in-your-Sleep."

Daniel looked at him then. The sight of the captain's own face reflected in the soldier's pupils may have given him some pause, for he seemed to release Daniel for a moment, but then tightening his pressure on him, he cried out with vehemence:

"I'm the only one left to you in this entire fucked-up world and you know it."

Rising over the soldier, he dropped his smartly creased crisp trousers, pulled away starched dazzlingly white shorts, and fell in furious stiffness and bulging agitation against Daniel's face, still holding the revolver in hand.

Once it was understood that Private Haws of Headquarters Squad was Captain Stadger's steady choice for "special detail," all the rules under which the enlisted man had lived in his squadron were suspended, and in effect no longer applied to him. He was now considered so "special" that, to tell the truth, he had been separated in effect, from the service. He was in Captain Stadger's own army.

Daniel's sergeant, a bony little fellow from Missouri, stared at him now with penetrating lack of understanding. "You was a good soldier, Haws. Hate to see you end up like this in one man's special detail."

His preferential treatment and his being "singled out" meant, Private Haws learned from those to whom it had leaked down from above, that he would not be shipped out with the rest of them at the end of their basic training. In all probability, he would stay on at this army post for the "duration," until the end of the war and perhaps of time itself.

"You done so good in everything," the sergeant went on,

considering Daniel's case. "You got a perfect record here, oh with a few exceptions, maybe." Here the sergeant looked at Daniel's cut-up face, which he ascribed to "harmless" brawls and fights in town. "Maybe, however," the sergeant ruefully continued, "the higher-ups will change things around after a bit and give you back to us." He looked off in the distance now, toward the Gulf, spat, wiped his mouth, stooped over and picked up some sand in his hands and rubbed the sand into his palm and fingers. "I seem to have caught myself a case of the itch down here, Haws," Sergeant Munsey said. "How do you feel about our God-damned South?"

"There wasn't too much up North for me." Daniel was laconic.

"You don't talk too much like a Northerner neither, sure enough, Haws." The sergeant studied his "lost" enlisted man. "But you don't talk like anybody I ever knew, come to think of it.

"Look," he drew the private now over to the back of his own tent, spoke to him almost tenderly. "This don't go beyond you and me now, keep in mind, but that captain you're under ain't no God-damned good. You got to get yourself out from under him, or he'll break your ass . . ."

The sergeant paused at the look this received from the enlisted man. Then he continued: "Stadger is more army than the army, the arrogant bastard. And he don't act like a captain or a general, he acts like God Almighty." He studied Daniel now closely. "You look bad, boy . . . Why don't you report for sick call?"

Daniel waved his hand dispiritedly, and the sergeant's eye rested briefly on the sheet of perspiration convering the private's brow.

"Remember our little talk here has been strictly on the

Q.T., Haws. But if you need me, I'll help you, Haws, if I can help."

As if unable even now to break away, the sergeant continued: "Stadger's got no right borrowing you from this outfit, from the whole God-damned army." He exploded angrily. Then, letting more sand trickle down between his fingers, he mumbled, "What can we do about it, though." He sighed. "Colonel swears by that cocksucker captain. You be on the Q.T. now about our little talk. After all, I'm married with a wife and kids' future to worry about," Sergeant Mursey seemed to shake off any plan of action, or correction of abuses. "Won't do any of us any kind of good to make the captain our enemy."

Captain Stadger had seen from the start out of the depths of his own being that Daniel Haws expected the trial and torture that was now to come. If the soldier had not at first precisely welcomed it, the captain knew that now at last his charge understood it was completely necessary and that it had always been fated to come.

Because the captain now had the letters containing the announcement of the death of Amos—the only real obstacle ever between them—the officer was certain that Daniel was more prepared than ever for complete surrender and submission.

Daniel knew hiding or concealment was no longer possible. As to running away from the camp into the world, a fugitive again, Daniel did not even consider such a move. He had run off before, and he had returned, as if indeed to and for Stadger. The latter had everything now which pertained to or was of Daniel Haws, he had everything "on" him and from him, and carried his whole life with him as no other person living or dead could or ever had; everything about the soldier was engraved in memory, on file, in Captain Stadger himself, his sole knower, judge, confessor, enemy, friend, and authorized executioner. Daniel knew at last he had come to that limit of life where no action on one's own part is possible or thinkable.

He heard a twig crack then, and the small bushes beside him move.

"Been gettin' impatient, I bet, Private Haws," he heard the familiar voice.

Daniel rose, made a slight motion with his hand against his forehead in way of salute.

His eye fell to the captain's belt from which hung a new addition, a sheathed knife, on which Stadger's hand rested somewhat emphatically. He smiled to note Daniel's attention to its presence.

If surprise was a state of mind of which the soldier was any longer capable, he was now surprised, for the captain ceremoniously removed his starched shirt, his hand-stitched undershirt (an almost feminine blue) and then, removing his knife from its sheath, began slashing his own chest with calm deliberation.

"Have some mercy then on yourself!" Daniel heard his own voice.

Tearing apart Daniel's own khaki covering, Stadger slashed his chest less savagely than he had his own, and pressing his own bleeding wound against Daniel, cried into the soldier's face:

"This is so there's not the slightest doubt in your mind I'll chicken out of any of this, or give you the damndest tiniest chance to chicken on me, until we're at the end of the road of all this . . ."

He pressed the soldier now with his rib case until Daniel collapsed in the captain's embrace.

In his extreme physical suffering, Daniel finally turned to his own torturer for sympathy. It was this action of the soldier that Captain Stadger himself now evidently required, in his own despair, for without Daniel's turning to him, he might not have been able to find the strength to inflict the last and most consummate of the punishments he had ready for the man elected for them.

Early that evening with his shock of black hair drenched from torment, Daniel leaned against the captain's chest, felt his breath as hot as from steel-mill furnaces, and heard Stadger in dulcet tones promise him keener pains that would subdue the ones he had suffered up until then.

"For you wouldn't want to stop now when your body has gone this far with me," he soothed his captive. "We must go through to the end now, Haws, to the absolute finish line."

Captain Stadger musing, dreamy, spoke of sharp iron, scythes, hooks and when he had tormented Daniel until both fell, without a stitch of clothing, into each other's arms like renowned athletes who have won some coveted wreath, the captain deposited Daniel carefully on a path covered with moss, and said he would show him now the weapon he had been saving for the final test and proof.

Stadger went to a clump of bushes, looked up briefly toward the low-hanging sky with its pulsating array of southern constellations, then bending dug in some leaves, carefully touched something.

Daniel lay unconscious, but the captain easily awakened him by a new show of exigency.

"I've hunted for this particular piece here for a long endless time," he pulled open Daniel's eyes with his fingers, and looked longingly in his pupils.

The captain was holding the weapon in front of Daniel now. When the soldier saw it, he recognized it as one of those immemorial instruments of destruction mentioned by his preacher reading from Scripture when as a boy he and his mother had attended the Disciples of Christ Church long ago.

In his own weak horror, he now held on to Captain Stadger's arm as one might to an anaesthetician who must accompany one to the shadows of death.

"I've been hunting all my life for the right man, the right body and will, who could accept this perfect weapon," Captain Stadger went on looking into the soldier's eyes. "Now I have them all."

They both lay then next to one another on the moss, near a row of the night-blooming moonflower, without a stitch to cover them, calm and collected.

"You didn't ask when it was to be," Captain Stadger complained softly, "so, Haws, I will tell you. It's tomorrow night, which is a Saturday. No moon, cloudy. Everybody'll be out on pass, nearly, just as if you and me was in this outpost together all by ourselves with nobody for miles, for our trial and experiment."

Daniel nodded, and let his hand rest on the captain's extended arm.

Perhaps his fever went down, or some last kind of instinctive animal prompting to save his body and life rose in Daniel. He now got up, determined to return to camp and seek help. Stumbling in the dim light of dawn, he fell across the outstretched form of the captain, and bending down was astonished to note again that without his garrison hat and uniform, wearing only his identification tag and an additional gold identification bracelet, stripped of any authority for the moment, Stadger looked scarcely older than himself. Sunk in heavy slumber, he had a harmless, almost cherubic appearance.

Grabbing his clothes and moving off a few yards from the sleeping officer, Daniel moistened his khaki handkerchief, wiped off the traces of blood around his nose and lips, and went as fast as he could to the sergeant's tent.

To his dismay he caught sight of Sergeant Munsey, already with his grip in hand, walking in the direction of the camp's exit.

Catching up with him, breathless, Daniel could say nothing for a moment.

"Still giving you a rough time, Haws?" Munsey studied his outlandish appearance and manner.

"I'd like to ask you that favor you promised me a while back," Haws got out.

The sergeant expressed impatience. His wife and kids were waiting for him at a hotel in New Orleans, Haws heard the words vaguely, and then something else about the camp bus waiting.

"I hear your pass is cancelled as per usual, Haws," the sergeant's voice reached him now again after a pause.

"Can't you call the Colonel on the phone before you go, sergeant?" Daniel blurted out.

The sergeant indicated the earliness of the hour by pointing to his wristwatch. Still studying Daniel's face, the noncom hesitated a moment. Looking down at his shoe, he lowered his small grip, bent over methodically to remove some white tooth paste which had fallen on the toe, then picked his grip up again.

"We can talk to the colonel next week about it," the ser-

geant was grave. "I mean it now, Haws. We'll see him together." He looked away quickly from Daniel's eyes.

"For Christ's sakes, Haws," he added, "nobody's going
to kill you, after all." The sergeant laughed.

He put his hand on Haws's shoulder, then gave him a
light friendly punch in the stomach and said goodbye.

Returning from the mess hall with his dirty mess kit,
Daniel put the aluminum plate and utensils into the dirty
soapy water of the first container, moved to the second pail
filled with clearer hot water, and then on to the third pail
full of furiously boiling clear water. Whether it was the
sudden contact with the fire under the containers of water
or a sudden upsurge of his fever, his face was suddenly
swimming with perspiration so that at first the sight of the
floating newspaper photo was unbelievable as a mirage. It
seemed to be Amos's face moving in the churning liquid.
He stood transfixed until another soldier yelled at him im-
patiently to move on. Placing his hand in the boiling water,
Daniel slowly drew out the paper, to the astonished outcry
of some soldiers near him, and unconscious of their horror
walked to a clump of bushes and half-fell down near a sand
pile.

As the newspaper began to dry slightly in the Gulf
breeze, he studied the face and saw that he had had no hal-
lucination.

Above the countenance of his lost Amos, who looked out
at him as from some non-existent eternity, was the heavy
black headline:

LAST RITES FOR SLAIN YOUTH

Some skin from his fingers damaged by the boiling water
had come off onto the newspaper held tight by him in both

hands. His head fell back against the pile of sand which he had used so frequently to scrub his mess kit.

"You can come past for me anytime now, Captain Stadger," he muttered.

23

The penmanship on that envelope and on the creased half-torn pieces of ruled letter-paper inside looked no more like Daniel's handwriting than if he had let a tame spider run over the page. It did not look like a communication formed by one human being for another. Eustace had paused a long time over it, after removing the letter from the mailbox.

Amos's terrible death, his own sickening feeling of responsibility for it, his involved correspondence with Cousin Ida, and his own growing despair made him now incapable of feeling further loss and tragedy, but he knew, even though Luwana Edwards claimed she had lifted from off him the Mantle of Second Sight, what the handwriting meant. He knew what was to come and he had no wish to confirm what he foresaw by reading it.

Not opening the letter that morning immediately, he gave one of his long essay-talks on letters, out of desperation, to Carla. "Letters," he began, "our wonderful postal service and its destiny-bearing carriers of the mails. Those scraps of paper disfigured with the juices of plants and insects which tell us of fate, love, and destruction, change the circulation of the blood and configuration of the brain as we read, while the postman is unaware, as he goes his rounds, that he carries the skeins of destiny in his leather pouch."

Carla took the letter from his hands.

"Is this the handwriting of that Negro psychic?" she asked. "You told me she had washed her hands of you after Amos died." Then she spied the Mississippi postmark.

She surprised Eustace by opening the envelope without permission. After all, her action seemed to say, she was in charge of everything now.

"Read me what he says, since you were indecent enough to open it," Ace told her.

Carla first read the message to herself. Then at his command she began, in her metallic business woman voice pronouncing the words aloud, but Eustace interrupted her suddenly.

"Can't you just tell me the gist of it, maybe, Carla, dear?"

A bit taken aback, she looked at the letter's single short paragraph again and said, "He simply says you're the only person in the world left to him now. He's ill with malaria."

Eustace asked then to see the letter. He stared at it, blinking.

"That's no more his hand than it's Jesus Christ's," he said.

Creeping back barefoot to where he had left the captain briefly, Daniel stood for a moment by a crape myrtle bush watching the sleeping terror that was the man who had come out of his worst expectations and dreams. Daniel pulled off his trousers and lay down next to the officer under one of the latter's extended arms, which even in sleep was tight with bundles of sinews. He lay sleepless through the rest of the night, while the intense heat made stinging salt drops of sweat fall from his own forehead and from the officer's arms and face into his eyes. He made no motion to wipe the sweat away. Every so often a moth or other night insect would light on his face to touch him with hairy appendages, and he allowed it to remain without motioning it away as the captain had that time, when the flies crawled over his face, pretended insensibility.

In the morning Daniel woke up alone. His fever had gone down some, and he hastened over to the medical officer's tent where he met Lieutenant Carrens. He was about to say, "I want to go on sick call," when the lieutenant anticipated him with, "Captain Stadger tells me he's going to drive you himself up to the hospital in Hattiesburg and let them check on your fever."

For a second or two he may have believed the lieutenant's statement. Then incredulous, and casting aside any thin hope he might have had, he turned away, knowing he would not try anything more to save himself. He went back into the deepest part of the underbrush without having tasted a thing in the mess hall.

As his fever rose now, he remembered going back a few times to the back of the mess hall and begging a cup of their heavy chicory coffee from the mess sergeant. Then the first thing he knew, it was again dark, with spots of heat lightning in the distance over the Sound.

Daniel waited now with the most extreme impatience for the reappearance of Captain Stadger, and sudddenly the terrible thought presented itself that perhaps the captain would not appear. He knew then that he counted greatly on the officer's coming, that he counted above all else on receiving whatever it was he was to receive finally from his hands, that he counted on the "release" by which Stadger would sever him from all and everything he had had connection with before. He waited now for the captain with the impatience with which he had waited, in his hidden soul, for Amos. He was ready and he was at full surrender.

As the evening wore away and there was no Captain Stadger, his fever mounted and he began to allow to escape from his throat certain cries almost like those of the longing a wild animal will emit for an absent mate. The flashes of summer lightning continued and were followed by shattering peals of thunder.

Then suddenly at last he saw the white figure coming toward him, and he gasped with relief.

Captain Stadger, however, had altered indefinably, one of his hands trembled slightly, and he sat down at a distance from Haws.

It was Daniel who went over to him.

"I'm ready to begin, sir," the soldier said.

"God damn this lightning!" The captain turned his face away from Daniel toward the Gulf, where the storm was originating.

A shrinking hesitancy and disappointment came over Daniel Haws's face, a real grief that the captain should show even token fear of anything, lightning or storm. It was this look of incipient but unmistakable reproach on Daniel's face that broke the spell and revived the real captain. Stadger stood up and went over to where the soldier faced him.

"Wipe that look off your face, Haws."

"We'll see if you fail me before I do you!" Daniel shot back at him.

When the captain still hesitated, Daniel muttered, "You yellow cocksucker."

The captain smashed his jaw with murderous thrust, knocking the soldier back against the oak tree.

Even though there was the crash again of thunder and more of the lightning which the captain evidently feared so much, the sight of the soldier's flowing blood snapped whatever hesitation may have held back the officer's hand. Quickly, like a man working fast to save a sinking vessel, Stadger stripped the enlisted man of the last of his clothing, tied him with the special wire to the tree. Daniel sighed vociferously. He had waited for death so long, he was almost already at peace, and the look of satisfaction on the soldier's face removed any last fear or compunction the captain may have had of elements, man, God.

"Tell me what I'm going to do to you?" Captain Stadger asked when he had securely tied him. The exhaustion of the last moments had cost the captain something, it was clear, and he spoke now with his head falling for the moment on Daniel's bare shoulder.

"Kill me," the soldier pressed his face against the captain's neck.

The captain struck him viciously again and again, and the queer sound as of bone breaking was faintly audible through the uproar of the tropical storm.

"Don't you command me, you fucker," the captain's voice rose.

Then he repeated his question to the soldier: "What am I going to do to you?"

"Have power," Daniel mumbled.

He struck the soldier again and again.

"Answer my Goddamned question right, Haws."

"You're going to exercise your rightful authority over me," Daniel whispered.

The captain was only partly satisfied.

"What more, Haws?"

"You're going to inflict punishment according to your orders," the soldier replied. Then in a wild delirium Daniel

Haws talked, lectured, ranted, quoted the Articles of War, rehearsed court-martial, confessed, condemned himself.

"How did you show Amos Ratcliffe your love?" Captain Stadger's voice came like the thunder behind them, while with pitiless savagery he held open the mutilated man's eyelids.

"I never gave him love," the soldier said. "I failed him as I failed myself."

Pulling out of his pocket a photograph of the dead boy, Captain Stadger thrust it in front of the soldier.

"Prefer me to him now, and you're free, Haws."

When Daniel did not reply, he rained one blow after another upon his prisoner until the bark of the tree ran red.

Leaving the soldier for a few moments then, he returned with the weapon he had shown him a short while before.

A pink sheet of lightning illuminated the weapon's sharp edges and the captain without a word more began his work, pushing like flame with the instrument into Daniel's groin upward and over, and then when its work was nearing completion he put his face to Daniel's and pressing said something, in bloody accolade, that not even Daniel heard.

About 2 A.M. on Sunday, Corporal Paulding, from the colored section of the encampment, said he heard a service revolver go off. As he later testified during the full investigation of the tragedy, after the shots, he saw to his never-fading horror a naked man emerge from the woods "carrying his bowels in his hands like provisions." The man fell in a pool of gore at his feet. He was not dead. They had been lucky to have an ambulance which, inexplicably, had already been brought to the entrance of the camp and in it, still conscious and crying, the soldier, Private Haws, had kept screaming all the way to hospital. "Kill me, kill me, for I've stood all tests, and you owe me my death."

They did not find Captain Stadger's body until the next afternoon—he had hidden himself so carefully in the place he had selected for shooting himself through the head with his service revolver.

epilogue

24

The series of terrible summer events had cleared Eustace's head and made his memory almost as crystal clear as before his marriage. Having bought his freedom—he liked to think by means of Amos's having earned the money in the park —the Mantle which had fallen onto him from Luwana Edwards was now snatched up and away from him. He realized that this not only was the conclusion of his youth but also the end of what he had thought he was. After these awful events, ending in the deaths of Amos and Daniel, he never wrote a line again.

Eustace, abdicating both as seer and poet, now found himself no longer the center of a group of disciples or even a "figure." While the "economic burnout" (in which horror he had somehow been an important person) modulated into a world war, he was merely Carla's husband.

It was, in any case, Carla's turn. She had been in the wings, and then to her own unbelief her cue came, and she walked out to the center of the stage. The bright lights showed her graying hair and all those lines, the ravages of bread-winning, poverty and disappointment. Having lost her role as the romantic love of any man, there she was, the star, after everyone else had left. She was frightened, but looking down at her hands, she saw she was steady.

Eustace's final abdication came as follows.

As he waited in the last days of summer for further word from Mississippi—he was as anxious to know the end of the Daniel-Amos story as a depraved inveterate novel-reader —to his own queer exhilaration and sick terror, his own draft number improbably came up. He smoked some of the marijuana Amos had left him some weeks before his death (it seemed incredible to him that he had not seen Amos alive now for at least six weeks). At the army induction center he was greeted by a pale professional doctor with the usual horror professionals often show when they meet someone alive in a different category of human existence than their own. Ace was about to tell the doctor he was a criminal degenerate, who had caused a boy's death, when the medic informed him there was every indication he had syphilis, and should be under a physician's care. He gave Eustace, to his grudging gratitude, a beauty of a pain-killer, which made him feel almost ready to go on living.

Able to get through the day now with his pain-killer and the marijuana supply, he spent the next two weeks quietly, during which he had begun to feel, in the wind from the east and the flying carpet of dead maple leaves on 55th Street, winter's touch and breath, when there arrived three communications in the mail.

The first was from the draft board, confirming the fact he was 4-F owing to venereal disease and traces of only partially cured tuberculosis.

The sight of the other two letters, also official, from the Army, one originating in New Orleans, made the hair on the back of his neck bristle. Not able to read these communications right away, he went into the bathroom, washed his face carefully, then shaved with the German straight razor Amos had bequeathed him, sat down, his ablutions completed, in an expensive dressing-gown, also out of Rat's effects from his "kept" period with Reuben Masterson.

It was about noon, he remembered, and looking out at the light coming from Washington Park and the rose garden, he felt he had skipped ten years somewhere. He felt he was an elderly man of forty.

After reading both of the government letters from the Army, he later tried to pretend to Carla that he could not remember where he had hidden them behind the torn wall-paper of his bedroom.

"Because you are the only person listed as related in any way to Private Daniel Haws, serial number 3603358," the first one began, "we wish to inform you of his condition. Private Haws was seriously injured while in basic training, at Camp Biloxi, and was transferred to this army headquarters hospital here in New Orleans. It is not certain he will be able to recover. The extent of his physical injuries are very serious, including abdominal lesions. . . . He has, even more seriously, shown extreme mental disturbance. As an enlisted man, he will receive every care and attention. If you know of any kin or relatives of the soldier, etc."

Opening the second official letter, Eustace read the single sentence which informed him that Private Daniel Haws had died of injuries sustained in basic training.

Somehow, with an ordinarily poor memory, Eustace Chisholm could recite the exact contents of those prosaically worded Army communications, while he would stumble if he recited Shakespeare or Virgil's lines, his favorite of all, as translated by Dryden:

I know thee, Love! in deserts thou wert bred,
And at the dugs of savage Tigers fed;
Alien of birth, usurper of the plains!

While Eustace tried to figure out whether he had been intended to be a writer and poet and had thrown away his
gift, or whether his wanting the Mantle returned to its original owner showed that he had never been meant to write
from the beginning—whatever the case, in the dead of
night, toward the beginning of November, he had got up
from sharing his bed with Carla, and had gone into the little
alcove where he kept the big pile of old newspapers on
which his poem was written.

"You'll catch your death!" Carla had cried to him.

Then she heard his screams.

What had happened was that, striking a match to find his
way, he had set the whole stack and binding of his works
into angry bursts of flame, which sprang at the same time
onto his expensive bathrobe.

Flinging a cotton blanket over him, Carla had managed
to put out the fire on his own person, and in her concern to
see whether he had seriously burned himself—they had
gone out into the kitchen to inspect his injuries—they did
not think of the burning poems themselves, until Carla
rushed out to them and found the papers ashes. Oddly
enough, a large spread of a long newspaper account, with co-
pious pictures of the wedding of Reuben Masterson and
Maureen O'Dell, remained partially intact.

Afterwards Eustace was sitting in a big "new" chair in
the kitchen which she had purchased from the Salvage,
from which he could more comfortably look down into the
alley.

"Can you bear to hear your poem is burned to nothing?" she inquired.

"I want to tell you something, Carla," he yawned.

She went over to him and put some pomade on his burned arm. "I'm listening, sweet," she said at a sigh of impatience from him.

There was no sound at all in the room just then until the wind caught the Woolworth glass chimes, and now they tinkled comfortingly.

"It's come over me too clear to back down, Carla, and I want you to know. You see how calm I am about the poem burning. I'm not a writer, that's my news, never was, and never will be," he told her.

"Furthermore you don't think I'm a poet and I know I'm not," he finished.

"I don't care what you accomplish, if anything." Carla pressed her head over his, looking back in the direction of the extinguished conflagration. "All I ever cared about was you."

Staring at her dumbly, he stirred, pulled her head down toward his mouth, covered her neck with silent kisses and then slowly, like all the sleepwalkers in the world, took her down the long hall to their bed, held her to him, accepted her first coldness as she had for so long accepted his, and then warmed her with a kind of ravening love.